Garden Norfolk 1550 – 1900

Edited by Tom Williamson and Anthea Taigel

Centre of East Anglian Studies

1990

Designed and Printed by the Printing Unit, University of East Anglia.

Preface

The Norfolk Historic Gardens Survey was jointly organised by the Centre of East Anglian Studies and Norfolk County Council, and funded by the Manpower Services Commission. The project, which ran from February 1988 to February 1989, was directed by ourselves (Tom Williamson and Anthea Taigel) and supervised by Michael Ball. This book contains some of its results. It is written by the members of the survey team, which also included Paul Farrow, Anne Kruyer, Tom McGeary and Robin Watson. The line drawings are by Paul Farrow, the photographs by Anne Kruyer and Robin Watson.

We would like to offer our thanks to R.G. Carter (Holdings) Plc for generously providing, and maintaining, a crew bus for the entire duration of the project. Thanks are also due to Judith Cantell of Norfolk County Council, for much help and advice; to Jack Pilgrim, of the University's Establishment Division, for getting the scheme off the ground; to Notcutts Ltd, for generous financial support; to the staff of the Norfolk Record Office, for much patience and assistance; and to A. Hassel Smith, George Carter, John Dixon Hunt, and Richard Wilson, for advice and encouragement. Special thanks are due to Liz Bellamy, who did the final copy-editing of the text.

We would also like to thank the following for permission to reproduce illustrations. The National Trust (Plate 3); Mr E.R.M. Pratt and the Norfolk Museums Service (cover illustration and Plate 2); the Bodleian Library, Oxford (Figure 8); the Norfolk Record Office (Figures 3 and 9); Lord Coke (Figure 9); Derek Edwards and the Norfolk Archaeological Unit (Figures 13 and 14); and Mr R.T. Bramley (Plate 7).

Above all, we would like to thank the owners of the parks and gardens investigated by the survey team. Without their kindness, cooperation, and hospitality none of this would have been possible. We would like to stress that the mention of any garden or park in this book does not imply that it is open to the public.

This is not intended as a definitive account of the history of gardens and parks in Norfolk, the study of which is still being continued at the Centre of East Anglian Studies. Rather, it is an interim statement, and in part a series of personal views, on particular aspects of the county's rich and varied garden heritage. More than anything else, this book is a tribute to hard work and enthusiasm of the survey team.

Contents

Chapter One
The Early Geometric Garden in Norfolk, c.1550 – c.1730

The earliest ornamental gardens known in England were 'formal' in their layout: that is, the paths, turf, and flower beds within them made up geometric, and often symmetrical, patterns. Such gardens went through a sequence of styles, resulting not only from changing fashions but also from a complex range of social, financial and practical factors. In addition, within any given period, there were considerable variations in size and form. Gardens such as those created by Henry VIII at Hampton Court, or by Isaac de Caus at Wilton, were extremes. Vast gardens like these were available only to the very wealthy, to members of the royal family or the court aristocracy. There was only a small number of these in the whole country, and they form a minute part of any county's garden history. Far more common were the gardens of the lesser aristocracy and gentry, about which comparatively little is known, and less has been written.

Early Walled Gardens

All gardens are composed of two very different elements: 'hard' and 'soft' landscaping. Hard landscaping is the term generally used for features made of inert materials, such as walls, garden houses, or gravel paths. Soft landscaping, in contrast, refers to the live elements of a garden, such as grass, hedges or trees. Nowhere in Norfolk can we find a garden which today appears as it did in the sixteenth or seventeenth centuries, for soft landscaping changes constantly, and the types of plants used in small gardens are relatively short-lived, compared with parkland trees. Hard landscaping, on the other hand, has a better chance of survival, and although most early walled gardens were destroyed as they went out of fashion in the eighteenth century, a few remain, as upstanding features or in earthwork form. From these, and from the evidence provided by maps and documents, we can learn something about the earliest Norfolk gardens.

Gardens of the sixteenth and seventeenth centuries were invariably enclosed, by walls, hedges, fences or dykes. Of these alternatives, walling required the least maintenance, but it was also the most expensive. The horticultural benefits of walls, however, made them the most popular form of enclosure. Not only did they provide a sheltered environment, and thereby extend the growing season, but in addition plants could be trained against them. Moreover, the walls could themselves add to the beauty and grandeur of a garden, for they were usually decorated with castellations, figured brickwork, arcading, gateways and various forms of coping.

One of the best examples of an early walled garden in Norfolk is at Besthorpe Hall near Attleborough. In common with a number of similar sites, the surviving structures are not all of one date, but have been altered and added to over many decades. The earliest enclosure lies to the south of the hall and probably dates from the late sixteenth century. It has three almost identical brick gateways, set centrally in the walls. All have round arches flanked by Ionic piers, and surmounted by a curious double circle 'bulls eye' motif (Figure 1). The Great Garden, which lies to the west of the hall, was probably built around the middle of the seventeenth century and, as its name suggests, was rather larger. Smaller, additional enclosures were built to the north of the house, and to the east, on the opposite side of the entrance drive. These are shown on an eighteenth-century map but, unfortunately, do not survive today. As with most Norfolk gardens in this period, there was no attempt to bring the additions into one overall symmetrical pattern.

The Great Garden at Besthorpe was originally terraced on all sides, and the terraces still survive as earthwork banks. Terraces were a feature of several sixteenth- and seventeenth-century gardens in the county: another fine example, still with its retaining wall, survives at Intwood. They would have provided a clear view of the geometric patterns of knots or parterres in the main area of the garden.   Several sixteenth- and seventeenth-century gardens in Norfolk contained ornamental buildings, but only a few survive. Some may have been used as 'banquetting houses', in which a 'banquet' or final course of a meal would be taken. One of the most impressive is at Kirby Cane (Figure 2). Of late seventeenth-century date, this fine building is three storeys high, has raised ornamental brickwork on the facades, a castellated top and rows of diamond-headed dove holes set into the top storey. Its size and detail suggest that it was once part of an equally elaborate garden, but only fragments of the contemporary walls survive. Another impressive garden house survives at Bawburgh, although here the hall has been demolished and the structure now stands, rather incongruously, between a housing development and a duck farm.

Figure 1: A sixteenth-century garden gate at Besthorpe Hall.

Figure 2: The late seventeenth-century garden house at Kirby Cane.

The proliferation of enclosed courts seen at Besthorpe was probably typical, and by the middle of the seventeenth century many large houses had a 'Great Garden', and a 'Little Garden', with other enclosures named after their principal use, such as the orchard, walnut ground, or nut yard. In these, aesthetics and practicality could be thoroughly mixed. Not all the enclosures, however, were completely walled. Some, especially orchards or kitchen gardens, were partly walled and partly hedged. This seems to have been the case with the most southerly enclosure at Besthorpe. Moreover, not all elaborately walled enclosures necessarily contained gardens. At Breckles, for example, the great walled courtyard in front of the house, with its elaborate and beautifully decorated gateway, is unlikely to have originated as a garden, although it encloses one now. Unlike the rather similar gates at Besthorpe, that at Breckles is wide enough for wheeled traffic, suggesting that the enclosure mainly functioned as an impressive entrance court for the house.

Great Gardens of the Seventeenth Century

Although most gardens in the county before the Restoration were of the small enclosed type, the county boasted at least two much larger layouts. Oxnead Hall, built by the Paston family in the sixteenth century, had, by the 1620s, one of the finest gardens in England (Plate 1). Like many other great gardens at this time, Oxnead was 'Italianate' in style: that is, its design was based on the kinds of gardens laid out around Renaissance villas in Italy, with terraces, fountains, and an abundance of statuary. The hall was built on an eminence overlooking the river Bure, and the large garden descended to the water in a series of terraces. The first terrace was reached from the level of the hall by 'flying steps' which descended either side of a bastion-like projection. At either end of this terrace, steps led down through archways to the second terrace – a large open area covering some 2,500 square metres, which was walled on the south and west. A magnificent Italianate arch was built at the southern end of the west wall, which still survives. To the east, this great parterre area was flanked by a terraced walk, which survives as a massive earthwork bank. On the far side of this, further to the east, was a second parterre area, apparently the same size as the first, and to the south of this was an elaborate series of ponds forming a water garden. The famous sculptor, Nicholas Stone, provided statues and a fountain for the Oxnead gardens in the 1620s. These have long disappeared from the site, but the fountain and a statue of Hercules were moved to Blickling in the eighteenth century and can be seen there today. The remains of the Oxnead garden are still impressive – in their heyday they must have been magnificent, and the cost, in terms of initial layout and subsequent maintenance, was no doubt enormous.

Oxnead was not the only great Italianate garden in the county. A similar, though apparently rather smaller garden was constructed in the late sixteenth century at Stiffkey, by Nathaniel Bacon. Here, too, the principal feature of the design was a series of terraces which provided a striking view across a river valley. The Stiffkey terraces are rather better preserved, and more massive, than those at Oxnead, and the remains of a summer house can still be seen at the end of the upper terrace.

At the same time as Nicholas Stone was working at Oxnead, a new hall was being built at Raynham, by Sir Roger Townshend. He, too, wanted his home to be embellished with imposing gardens, but the style he chose was rather different. The Raynham gardens, which covered an area of around ten acres (about four hectares), had few of the Italianate features seen at Oxnead or Stiffkey. Instead, they seem to have been influenced by current fashions in the Low Countries, an area with which Sir Roger had many contacts. Although the new hall was built above the valley of the river Wensum, no attempt was made to terrace the valley side. The layout of the garden was strikingly geometric. The main area consisted of a rectangle, divided into symmetrical sections. The hall lay within this area, forming an integral part of the geometry, and was flanked on three sides by gardens. This is a plan hard to parallel in England, but strikingly similar to the arrangement of the house and gardens at Honselaarsdijk, near The Hague, which were under construction at this time. Also reminiscent of Dutch gardens were the hedge-lined paths set with standard trees, which were a prominent feature of the Raynham design.

Oxnead, Stiffkey, and Raynham were rarities and, although there are some tantalising indications of a few other designs of comparable size, most Norfolk gardens seem to have remained small and enclosed until the last decades of the seventeenth century.

The Late Seventeenth Century

By the end of the seventeenth century, larger gardens were becoming more common, and our ideas about their appearance are rather less sketchy, since several were drawn or painted. Four illustrations, two executed in the 1680s and two around 1700, serve to show how varied the gardens of this period could be. Ryston Hall (Plate 2) was built by Sir Roger Pratt in the late seventeenth century. He designed the house and probably the gardens as well. Ryston had three main gardens: ornamental gardens in front of the two main facades, and a kitchen garden to the east. Each was walled, each had decorated gateways set centrally into the walls, and was divided by paths into four equal squares. In the south garden, the paths were of gravel and surrounded four grass 'plats', or lawns. In the centre of each plat was a circular bed, with a specimen conifer surrounded by flowers. The north garden had four grass plats with wide flower borders and beds, separated by grass paths.

An undated painting of Aylsham Old Hall (Plate 3) gives the impression of a more sophisticated, yet rather simpler garden. Here, too, grass plats predominated, but there is no trace of flowers or trees. There were three main walled gardens, all connected by decorated gateways and internally symmetrical, but each very different in shape and size. The largest lay to the west, and consisted of grass plats with cross paths, with a statue at their intersection. The garden in front of the house, in contrast, contained only two large grass plats divided by a central gravel walk. The third garden, to the east of the house, was only walled on two sides, and contained a garden house with a view over a long, narrow canal. Another area, to the north of the house, contained trees, and was probably an orchard.

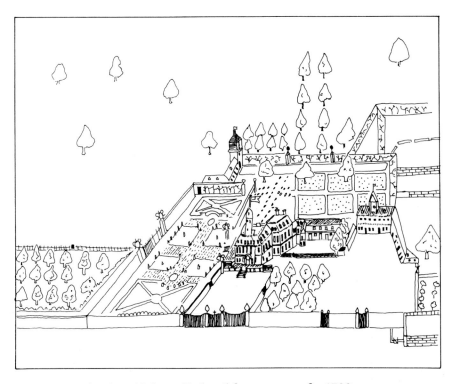

Figure 3: Buckenham Tofts Hall: detail from a map of c.1700.

13

The gardens at Buckenham Tofts are shown in a perspective view on the edge of a map, probably drawn up around 1700 (Figure 3). Two rectangular walled gardens formed the main ornamental layout, both approached directly from the house which, like that at Aylsham, was built on a terrace. The eastern garden, to the rear of the house, had six grass plats, some set with trees, gravel paths, and a long canal, stretching the width of the garden. Pleached trees lined the walls, and a three-storey garden house, possibly the converted tower of the redundant parish church, was positioned at the end of the canal. The main garden lay to the north of the house. It was much larger and more ornate. Walled on four sides, the walling was broken by gates, allowing a view into the surrounding meadows. This garden was divided into three areas of roughly equal size. The west and east of these had an identical layout, involving a square plat cut diagonally by paths. The central area was divided into four by straight paths. Each of the sections was bordered by geometric topiary, and each had a clipped shrub at its centre.

Some time in the late 1670s, Sir Jacob Astley began to build a new hall at Melton Constable, and either at the same time, or soon afterwards, an

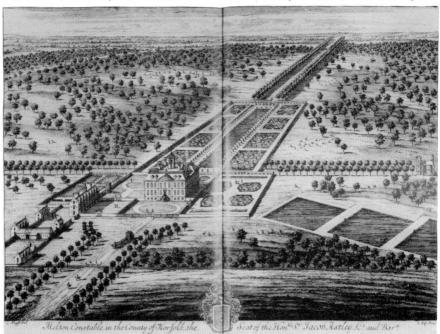

Figure 4: Melton Constable Hall, from Johannes Kip and Leonard Knyff, *Britannia Illustrata* **(1707).**

impressive series of walled gardens was laid out around it. In 1707, these were illustrated by Leonard Knyff and Johannes Kip in their collection of engravings entitled *Britannia Illustrata* (Figure 4). The engraving shows that the north entrance court and the east court were simple affairs of grass and gravel. This simplicity was not, however, maintained in the complex design of the rest of the gardens, which involved clipped shrubs, ornate geometric beds and a long canal aligned on the south front of the house. The axis of the canal was extended as an avenue through an adjoining deer park and out into the surrounding countryside.

The Axial Avenue Plan

Sites of the scale and magnificence of Melton Constable or Buckenham Tofts were still rare in Norfolk in 1700. But there is some evidence that even the gardens belonging to the minor gentry were increasing in size in the late seventeenth century. Perhaps more importantly, it would appear that aesthetic features were beginning to be established in the areas outside the garden walls. The clearest evidence of this is the appearance of avenues, focussed on the main facades of the house, extending out across the surrounding fields (Plate 4). Because most houses were built facing south, such avenues were usually oriented north/south. Many ran for considerable distances: at Rougham, the lime avenue planted in the 1690s was nearly a mile long (Plate 5). The axial avenue became the determining element in many gardens, and parterres and other features were often arranged symmetrically on either side. Minor avenues might be laid out on a cross axis, but they were comparatively insignificant features. Variations on this 'axial avenue plan' were immensely popular in Norfolk in the late seventeenth and early eighteenth centuries, both for the homes of the local gentry, and for larger houses. As the late as the 1730s, such layouts were still being created around impressive new houses like Langley Hall.

The Late Geometric Garden

As the fashion grew for larger and larger gardens, it became less easy to surround them with walls, because of the high cost of brickwork. Once colonisation of the surrounding landscape by ornamental features began in earnest, walls became obsolete as a part of the aesthetic garden, although still important in kitchen gardens because of their horticultural benefits. As landowners incorporated more of the surrounding land into their pleasure grounds, walls only interrupted views and vistas. The expense of maintaining intricate parterres and topiary was also proving prohibitive as gardens became larger, and thus planting became simpler. These factors

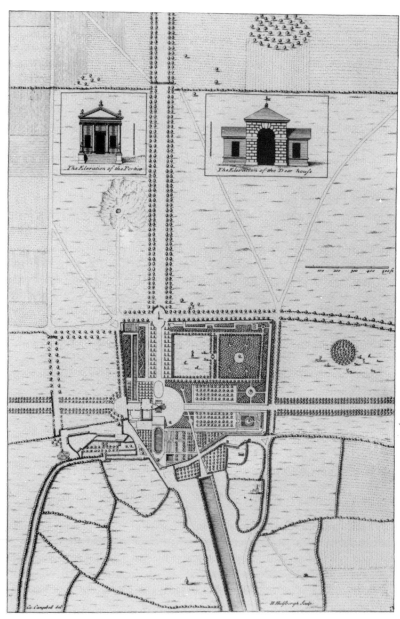

Figure 5: The gardens at Narford Hall, from Colen Campbell, *Vitruvius Britannicus* (1725).

16

taken together resulted in a new type of geometric garden, in which walling was excluded and in which internal divisions were formed by the cheaper and much more adaptable hedges and trees.

A plan of the garden and landscape at Narford, the seat of Sir Andrew Fountaine, was made by Colen Campbell in 1721 (Figure 5). Illustrations of the same site by Humphry Prideaux, made a few years later, allow us to get a good impression of what the garden would have looked like on the ground. These illustrations show extensive single and double avenues, either forming the limits of the garden or axially aligned on the house, crossing and recrossing the surrounding fields. A long tree-lined canal also extended into the landscape. This was not axially aligned on the house, for in this type of garden, overall symmetry had become far less important than it had been in gardens of the Melton Constable type, although geometry and regularity were still retained.

Within the garden, close-cut hedges, some regularly lined with standard trees, surrounded a number of different geometric elements, including groves (areas of ornamental woodland), canal gardens, and a maze. Classical temples and statues provided focal points, and straight gravel walks led from one area of the garden to another. Clipped shrubs lined some of these paths, or were regularly spaced around the perimetre of square lawns. While flowers would undoubtably have been planted, beside walks and around specimen trees in the groves, the main emphasis of the design was on trees and water. Maintenance costs would still have been high — gravel walks still needed to be weeded and rolled and hedges needed clipping. But some of this cost could now be offset by the value of the wood and timber which was being grown within the garden area. Groves were coppiced in cycles and the small wood produced could be utilised on the estate. Larger standard trees were seen as an investment, and at appropriate times could be removed without destroying the overall layout of the gardens.

Narford was not the only large garden of this type in Norfolk in the early eighteenth century. Horace Walpole wrote in his *Essay on Modern Gardening*: 'One of the first gardens to be planted in this simple but still formal style, was my father's at Houghton. It was laid out by Mr Eyre, an imitator of Bridgeman'. Another Colen Campbell illustration reveals that Houghton, too, was dominated by geometric elements — formal rides, vistas, avenues and groves — making up a layout even more intricate and extensive than that at Narford. Elements of this looser geometric style are also known to have been adopted at a number of other sites, including

Raynham, Blickling, Wolterton, and Gunton.

Not everyone, however, was prepared to give up their walled gardens and parterres, and the number of people who could afford to take several acres of land out of use to plant a wilderness or grove was, in any case, relatively limited. Some people bowed to fashion with reluctance, and others, even major landowners, refused to do so at all during this period. Melton Constable still had its walled geometric gardens in the late 1720s, and among the lesser gentry, as we shall see, walled gardens remained popular right through the second half of the eighteenth century, when the 'natural' landscapes of Lancelot 'Capability' Brown were the dominant elite fashion.

The larger, looser geometric layouts also took longer to disappear than some writers suggest. They were still being maintained, and even created, in the 1760s. When Brown was asked to prepare a scheme for Langley in 1765, his plans show that the the geometric wilderness flanking the avenue to the north of the house still existed. At Hillington, plans for a geometric grove, complete with a yew temple and a mount, were being drawn up in the early 1760s, although whether this scheme was ever executed is unclear. We are learning that we should not exaggerate the speed of the demise of the geometric garden in eighteenth-century Norfolk.

Chapter Two
Parks and Gardens in the Eighteenth Century

The Origins of Parkland

English parkland is a simple yet distinctive kind of landscape, consisting of individual trees and small blocks of woodland scattered irregularly, 'naturally', across a great expanse of grass. Sometimes the composition includes a serpentine lake, and the whole design is often bounded, in whole or part, by a belt of trees (Figures 6 and 7). It is often suggested that landscapes like this first appeared in England in the middle decades of the eighteenth century, the invention of great designers like William Kent and

Figure 6: Typical Norfolk parkland at Blickling.

Capability Brown. According to this view, the landscape park was the culmination of the trends described in the previous chapter, in which the enclosed geometric layouts of the seventeenth century were gradually extended and simplified. At gardens like Houghton or Narford, the wall was replaced by the sunken fence, or 'ha ha', and according to Horace Walpole 'no sooner was this simple enchantment made, than ... the garden in its turn was to be set free from its prim regularity, that it might assort with the wilder country beyond'. In the landscape park, this 'naturalising' process was taken a stage further, and by the 1760s and 1770s both walled gardens and the larger, more open geometric layouts had become unfashionable. In their place, an irregular, 'natural' landscape of grass and trees swept right up to the walls of the country house.

Figure 7: Typical Norfolk parkland at Bayfield.

There is a great deal of truth in the conventional account, but it is also slightly misleading. Areas called 'park', consisting of pasture irregularly scattered with timber trees and woodland, were not entirely new in the eighteenth century. They had been a feature of the English landscape since the time of Domesday. In the Middle Ages, a 'park' had been an enclosure serving as a venison-farm and hunting reserve, although with some subsidiary economic functions such as grazing for livestock, and timber and wood production. These early parks had seldom formed the setting for great country houses. Some ran up to the backs of their owner's homes, but many were located miles away – although they usually contained a lodge, providing temporary accommodation during hunting trips, as well as permanent accommodation for the ranger, who maintained the park and its deer.

In the late medieval period, there was a drastic decline in the number of parks in Norfolk, partly for economic reasons. The few which survived were, significantly, those attached to large houses. Melton Constable is one example, and Kip and Knyff's engraving (Figure 4) shows the great house and its geometric gardens partially surrounded by the irregular, sweeping landscape of the park. Deer parks began to be created again during the late seventeenth and early eighteenth centuries, but always now in the vicinity of a country house. New parks appeared beside the mansions at Buckenham Tofts, Kimberley, Raynham, Houghton, and elsewhere.

Yet in the seventeenth and early eighteenth centuries, the function of parks was slowly changing. They were beginning to be used for more than just hunting. Avenues began to be planted through them, bringing them into the same aesthetic scheme as the geometric gardens. Garden buildings were constructed within them, as at Hunstanton where, some time during the seventeenth century, the 'Octagon' – an elaborate moated summer house – appeared in the heart of the park. Indeed, by the early eighteenth century, deer were no longer being regularly hunted within parks, although they were culled.

Moreover, the concept of the 'park' was becoming wider, and was loosing its specific association with deer. Thus, in a few places during the course of the seventeenth century, landowners found that they could no longer afford to maintain a herd of deer. Yet the park beside the house was not disparked – that is, subdivided by hedges, or ploughed. Instead, the distinctive parkland landscape was maintained, although the area was now stocked with cattle or sheep. This, at least, appears to be what happened at Hedenham, Costessey, and perhaps elsewhere. Even more interesting is the appearance, during the 1720s and 1730s, of entirely new areas of 'park' adjacent to country houses which were never, apparently, stocked with deer, as at Merton (shown on an estate map of 1733) and Mannington (illustrated on a map of 1742).

Parks were, therefore, not an invention of the mid eighteenth century: they had long been an important component of the country house landscape. Yet their role changed as the century progressed. They became, not simply an appropriate accessory for a great house, but its only proper setting. The *à la mode* eighteenth-century country house should stand free of walled

21

gardens, geometric groves, avenues and the like, surrounded by an informal 'natural' landscape. More importantly, there was a vast increase in the number of parks in the decades after 1760. Parks ceased to be restricted to the estates of the greatest landowners: they descended the social scale, to become the normal possession of every local squire. By the 1790s, according to William Faden's map of Norfolk, there were no less than 117 parks of twenty hectares or more within the county, and anybody with any pretensions to gentry status had their house set within a landscape park, rather than within geometric gardens.

But although the landscape parks resembled, and were in part modelled on, the traditional deer park, there were certain marked differences. For the landscape parks did not usually contain deer, and their form was determined by aesthetic ideas, rather than just by their use.

Making Parks

Although continuing in broad terms the traditional deer park landscape, the design of the late eighteenth-century park went through a number of phases, which are discussed in more detail in chapter three. It is important to stress, however, that although books on garden history often read as catalogues of great designers, few Norfolk parks were designed by anybody famous. Although Kent, Brown, Richmond and Repton all worked in the county, the vast majority of parks were created by local designers, estate gardeners, or the owners themselves. Of the 117 parks shown on Faden's map, only twenty were worked on by designers of national importance. National styles were, in time, taken up with enthusiasm in the county, but specific designs were created by local people.

Members of the gentry learnt the accepted the rules of landscape design in a number of ways. Fashions and ideas were transmitted through illustrations and books, but visits to other people's parks, both in Norfolk and elsewhere, were also important. Diaries and travel journals make it clear that tours of parks and gardens were a major part of any itinerary. James Coldham of Anmer, for example, went on a tour of the north of England in 1752, and visited not only large and well-known sites like Studley Royal and Castle Howard, but also less famous places. At Seaton Delavel in Durham he visited Delavel House, and noted that 'the gardens are very moderate, some stone sheep plac'd up and down, which would deceive almost anybody till very near them'. An account of a tour of the West country in 1778, written by a member of the Rolfe family, describes the time it took to go round different

22

parks. Mrs Parker's garden and park at Saltrens in Devon 'is well worth seeing ... It will take about two hours to see the whole'. Mount Edgecombe, in contrast, was so extensive that 'it will require four hours', because the walks around the park 'may be four or five miles'. The writer adds that 'if there are any Ladies of the Party, on application to Lord or Lady Edgecombe, or in their absence to the Gardiner the night before, the Ladies may be accommodated with a one-horse chaise'.

Creating a park was a costly and complicated business, which involved a judicious combination of preservation, destruction, and addition. The first necessity was to have a continuous block of land, and among the minor gentry this might involve years, even decades, of purchase and exchange. Even when a parish was already owned in its entirety by a single individual, emparking still involved some reorganisation of the farms on an estate. Thus at Docking William Becher, estate manager for the Ffolkes family, wrote in 1804 that the lord of the manor, Christian Hare, 'has a plan for taking land from Barker and his other tennants, to make his own occupation more Parkish if I may be allowed the term, about his house to west, south and east'.

Once a block of land of sufficient size had been obtained, all signs of human activity, and of normal agricultural pursuits, had to be excluded from within it. This might involve the removal or alteration of settlements, although this was far less common in Norfolk than it was in some Midland counties. For in the Midlands, manor houses were often closely associated with compact villages, whereas, in most parts of Norfolk, settlement was more widely dispersed, so that parks could often be laid out in areas which were not already cluttered up with farms and cottages. Only a few villages are known to have been substantially altered or destroyed by park-making in the county – Houghton, Holkham, and Anmer are the most prominent examples. In all these cases, the village was eventually rebuilt on the edge of the park, as a feature of the estate landscape, and the parish church was left isolated within it.

Yet if such drastic alterations to the pattern of settlement were rare, less dramatic changes were quite common. At Letton, for example, a number of small farms and cottages scattered along the edge of Letton Green were removed when the park was laid out in the 1780s. But far more common than the removal of dwellings was the termination or diversion of public rights of way. Indeed, this almost always occurred when the larger parks were created. Landlords could not, however, simply close a public road at a whim. The correct legal procedures had to be followed. Initially, this involved the issue of a writ of *Ad Quod Damnum* in the Court of Chancery, a process which, in effect, asked the Crown and local proprietors whether their interests were adversely effected by the proposed change. This process was complicated, and involved quite a lot of money. At Heacham, for example, the lawyer's bill for calling the writ was £30.3.10. After 1773, however, a rather different proceedure came into force, as a result of a Parliamentary Act. Two local magistrates simply had to agree to the alteration. Having examined the road or footpath in question, they signed a Road Closure Order, which included both a map and a description of the right of way to be closed or diverted. This usually states that the old road is inconvenient, or superfluous to the needs of the local community; never that it stands in the way of the park-making schemes of someone who was, as often as not, a neighbour or friend of the magistrates concerned!

Although closed to the public, such roads did not always entirely disappear from the landscape. Often the line of the old road − which had usually run past the front door of the great house − survived as one of the principal entrance drives. Sometimes the line of a closed road is still visible in the park as a wide gully or 'hollow way' − as, for example, at Great Melton, where the line of the road closed by an order of 1776 survives as a prominent earthwork running through the southern area of the park. The provision of replacement roads was a major item of expenditure when parks were created: at Heacham, for example, the new road was less than a kilometre long, but £28.2.0 was spent on preparing its route, £48.11.6 on construction materials, and an unknown amount on labour.

In the eighteenth century, writers on landscape design often referred to the need to consult 'the genius of the place'. They argued that the topography of an area had to be carefully examined in order to understand the potential for improvement. To this end, a plan of the site was often drawn up prior to emparking, although few of these plans have survived. A map of Ditchingham, dated 1764, seems to be one of the few. It shows the area around the hall, including the two avenues and the formal walled gardens stretching down to the Broome Beck. The surveyor, in a marginal text, described the contours of the valley and the gradient of the stream, which was to be dammed to form a lake, and noted how the map showed the more 'remarkable trees', both in the avenue and 'on the hills at a distance'. Some of these were to be retained when the landscape was transformed into a landscape park.

The creation of a park generally involved the utilisation of existing features, especially trees. Many parkland trees began life as hedgerow timber, as Mike Ball discusses in chapter six, and maps surveyed in the eighteenth and nineteenth centuries often show parkland trees standing in suspiciously straight lines! But nevertheless, we should not underestimate the number of alterations and additions made as the new landscapes were created. Parks must, for a few years, have been scenes of intense activity. Heacham is a particularly well-documented site, for here the owner, Edmund Rolfe, kept a detailed account of the 'Various Expenses in the Improvements at Heacham begun in 1768'. In the first years, most of the expenditure went on diverting the road, putting in fencing, 'taking up trees and fences', and moving earth. As time went on, increasing amounts of money were spent on the purchase and carriage of trees, some of which came from Mr Aram's nursery in Norwich, some from Mundford, and some from Houghton. In October 1773, the construction of the ha ha was recorded in a series of entries:

Making a sunk fence	£17.0.0
Nails for ditto	£3.17.9
To oak posts, nails, and paling for ditto	£32.18.3
Carpenter for ditto	£3.18.6
In all, a total of	£40.14.6.

Work continued on the park for eight years, until 1775, by which time it had cost Rolfe £913.5.1. It is difficult to put this sum into context, but some idea of its magnitude can be gained by comparing it with the £14 *per annum* paid to Rolfe's gardener at this time. On the other hand, it is worth remembering that this sum was spread over eight years, during which time Rolfe's annual income seems to have varied between £1,200 and £2,320. Moreover, the money expended on the park has to be compared with that spent on other projects at Heacham during the 1760s and 1770s. As the park was being completed, work began on the construction of a new kitchen garden. A survey of 1773 shows that this covered no more than 1¼ acres, but the accounts reveal that it was incredibly expensive, costing nearly as much as the entire park to construct and equip – £898.7.0. Nearly half of this sum went to pay for the 481,000 bricks used in the walls and greenhouse. Moreover, as soon as the park and garden were completed, work began on the construction of the new hall, which continued until 1780. This cost no less than £4,128.1.4.

In short, although parks were expensive to construct, they were much cheaper than an equivalent area of geometric garden, and well within the means of most members of the local gentry by the end of the century. Indeed it could be argued that the most important feature of the informal 'landscape' park was that it supplied a cheap way of marking out large areas as ornamental and, ostensibly at least, as divorced from agricultural production. The result was an extensive, private, insulating space, which served to isolate the homes of the landed elite from local communities. By showing their knowledge of the correct stylistic rules, local landowners were also able to display to the world at large that they were members of polite society, appropriate rulers of the local community. Parks became the quintessential symbols of gentility, echoing in their design the ancient aristocratic landscape of the deer park. Yet they could be created at remarkably little expense. This, perhaps, is the secret of their popularity. But not only were parks cheap to create. They were also cheap to maintain, requiring only regular grazing by sheep and cattle. Indeed, income could be derived from this, and also − as discussed elsewhere in this book − from the systematic commercial exploitation of the woods and plantations which lay within, and encircled, the parkland.

Where Did All the Flowers Go?

According to most arbiters of fashion in the second half of the eighteenth century, the park should sweep uninterrupted to the main facade of the mansion. There was little place in this kind of landscape for flowers, flower beds, or the geometric layouts of paths which had characterised the kinds of designed landscapes described in chapter one. But some writers advocated a more modest approach. Horace Walpole, for example, suggested that the 'total banishment of all particular neatness immediately about a house, which is left gazing by itself in the middle of a park, is a defect', and 'whenever a family can purloin a warm and even an old-fashioned garden from the landscape designed for them by the undertaker of fashion, without interfering with the picture, they will find satisfactions on those days that do not invite strangers to come and see their improvements'. In Norfolk, it seems, many memebrs of the gentry would have agreed. Letters and diaries leave little doubt that walled gardens were regarded with real affection by many members of the gentry throughout the second half of the eighteenth century, and some people had very mixed feelings about their destruction. In 1776, for example, Beeston St Lawrence Hall was visited by Richard Hulton, brother-in-law of the owner, Jacob Preston. At the time, the grounds were being modernised by the landscape designer Richmond, but Hulton was unimpressed. He wrote in a letter to his sister:

> Mr Preston had one of the Gentleman Improvers here to modernise his grounds and is busy levelling his lawns, removing Gardens, walls and trees and laying down a new Kitchen Garden more remote from the house. It would grieve you if you were here to have such a fine kitchen garden cut up ... and laid in a lawn, but so it must be, our ideas are more extensive than those of our ancestors. They were cribbed up in small appartments, and sat on little cane chairs admiring the pretty inclosed garden edged with box and yew trees. We now indulge in elbow chairs, in appartments 20' by 30' by 15' high, and must extend our view over improved grounds as far as the eye can see without a disagreeable object intervening.

It is not surprising, then, to discover that walled enclosures were often maintained, against the tide of fashion, well into the second half of the eighteenth century, and sometimes beyond. The personal papers of James Coldham of Anmer Hall record how in 1775 he 'began to take Down the Walls in order to Finish my garden'. But this demolition was not the prelude to the creation of a fashionable landscape park, as we might expect, for Anmer park did not come into existence until the early 1790s, after Coldham's death. In reality, this new garden was an extension to the existing walled courts, for in 1782, Coldham described the fruit trees growing against the walls of 'The Wall'd in Garden' and the 'Flower Garden', and in April 1777 Coldham records, among other purchases made at Cambridge, 'Garden seeds − flowers'. At some places, owners never gave up their old walled gardens, and simply ignored the dictates of fashion, as at Intwood, where examination of the walls of the garden, together with estate maps, indicates that the garden was maintained, reconstructed, and even extended throughout the eighteenth and nineteenth centuries. Usually, however, such gardens were eventually swept away to make way for the new parkland landscape, often as young heirs, keen to display their awarness of fashion, inherited estates.

But once the parkland landscape finally triumphed, flowers did not simply disappear. As Barry Doyle argues in chapter five, their cultivation and display continued, but within the separate unit of the walled kitchen garden. As Repton noted, in praise of kitchen gardens: 'there are many days in winter when a warm, dry, but secluded walk, under the shelter of a north or east wall, would be preferred to the most beautiful but exposed landscape: and in the spring ... some early flowers and vegetables may cheer the sight'. Walled enclosures might seem ugly and unacceptable in the context of the parkland landscape; but the interior of the kitchen garden could be a place with its own particular appeal, after the destruction of other enclosures around a country house.

Chapter Three
The Aesthetics of Norfolk Parks in the Eighteenth Century

The Early Landscape Garden

When, in the early eighteenth century, young gentlemen returned from their expeditions abroad on the fashionable Grand Tour, they brought back not only impressions gained from Alpine and Mediterranean scenery, but also mementos of their visits in the form of paintings. These became important references for what an ideal landscape should look like. Claude Lorraine, a seventeenth-century French painter, was especially popular. His works depict idyllic Italian country scenes set against a background of trees, hills, sea and sky. The importance of horizontal dimensions is a marked feature of his work, and views were generally divided into fore-, middle- and background. The effect is one of light sweeping across a vast panorama, drawing attention to clear detail in the foreground, while the distant view becomes hazy and indistinct.

It does not seem to have been usual in the seventeenth century for writers or designers to make a connection between scenery and painting. But when, from the early eighteenth century, the landed rich began to mould the environment to a specific design, a major influence on their aesthetic predilections were the principles of composition derived from landscape painting. In the 1720s and 1730s, Charles Bridgeman and William Kent began to open up gardens to the surrounding world, and used principles of perspective, and of light and shade, to accentuate the visual qualities of the scenes they created. Their designs were considered 'natural', in contrast to the rigidly geometric gardens of the previous era, although Bridgeman's designs for Wolterton (Figure 8) and Gunton, and Kent's for Holkham (Figure 9), still display many geometric features. The influence of the landscape paintings was manifested in the tendency to conceive the park not as a single entity, but rather as a series of composed pictures, or views, which had to be seen from a particular perspective. Thus at Wolterton the dominant feature of the design was a vista, framed by plantations, out across lawn and lake to the distant wooded slopes around Blickling.

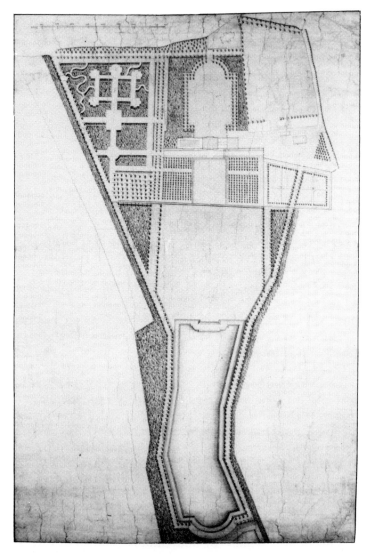

Figure 8: Plan of the gardens at Wolterton Hall, attributed to Charles Bridgeman, c. 1728.

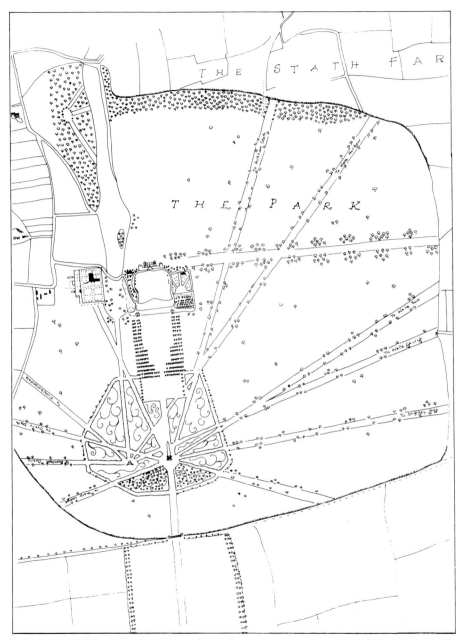

Figure 9: Holkham park and gardens, from an undated mid eighteenth-century estate map.

The use of framed views was more complicated at Holkham. Here, a mid eighteenth-century map shows a large number of rides and avenues, focussed on the semi-formal grove on the hill in the south of park. These were aligned on distant features in the landscape: villages, towns and prominent hills. Thus the vistas framed composed views, and on the map the main feature of each is indicated by a label. One avenue is directed 'to Stiffkey Hills', another 'to Wells Town', and so on (Figure 9). Holkham was visited in 1778 by Sylas Neville, when this arrangement was still partially in existence. He noted in his diary:

> The lake with its hanging woods & Holkham Church on the hill by much the finest objects seen from the house or grounds. Look back from a high bank to Holt. View of Cley & the sea between two banks on the right. View of Wells & the sea.

A more important aspect of the paintings that influenced landscape design was the frequent presence of ruins and classical buildings. Many early eighteenth-century landscapes had buildings inspired by those of the paintings, often functioning as key elements in framed views, and intended to evoke particular emotions. At Houghton, the Water Tower, a water supply reservoir for the house carefully disguised as a Roman temple, stands at the end of a major avenue. Holkham has its temple and obelisk, key points in the framework of avenues which divided the park, while at Blickling another temple, constructed in the early eighteenth century, still stands at the end of the main axial walk. Such buildings were not always classical in form: at Houghton, the parish church of St.Martin, isolated in the park after the surrounding village had been removed by Sir Robert Walpole, was restored in 1727 in a suitably 'gothick' manner, and became a feature of the parkland landscape.

Some quite small gardens had notable classical buildings. At Docking a temple stood at the end of an avenue reaching across the small park. At one time there was also a Hermitage here, as Arthur Young records in his *Six Week Tour through the Southern Counties*, published in 1764. It was located within one of the plantations and was created by adapting a small, two-roomed cottage. One room was lined with oyster shells, carpeted with pebbles and had a chimney-piece of grotto shellwork. This room contained the hermit's bed. The other was 'curiously wainscotted', with a ceiling 'decorated in a rustic manner, with scrolls and festoons of seaweed, deal shavings and painted ropes, in a gothic but very neat taste'.

PLATE 1: The early seventeenth-century garden arch, Oxnead.

PLATE 2: Ryston Hall, from a painting of c.1680.

PLATE 3: Aylsham Old Hall, from a painting of c.1690.

PLATE 4: Horstead Hall and gardens, from an estate map of 1699.

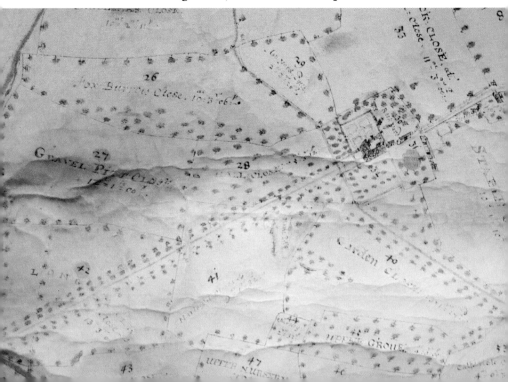

Many early eighteenth-century garden buildings have disappeared, like the three temples which stood within the elaborate gardens at Narford Hall. Sometimes their disappearance may be connected with the cheapness of their construction: the pyramid at Raynham, for example, has vanished without trace, but this is hardly surprising considering it was constructed entirely of wood.

The Brownian Park

Classical buildings and other references to antiquity were a characteristic feature of Norfolk parks and gardens designed between 1720 and 1750. Their use declined thereafter, although never entirely: Capability Brown, for example, 'gothicised' a seventeenth-century garden building in Melton Constable park and used it as a prominent feature in his design (Figure 10). But as more space was acquired by landowners, the idea grew that moods and emotions should be aroused by the manipulation of the landscape itself, rather than through the allusive power of structures and buildings. The landscape might still be framed as a composed picture, or a series of such pictures. But the pre-eminent aim was to create something which looked entirely 'natural'. As the Frenchman Francois de la Rochefoucauld, who travelled through Norfolk in 1784, put it: 'one might well attribute the lay-out of the English parks to nature'. But in his writings, the dichotomy between what constitutes 'a pleasant village' and 'unattractive countryside' is established with an emphasis on the *creation* of a *natural* scene.

Rochefoucauld was in no doubt about who was the most important creator of such scenes, commenting that 'since England has existed she has counted only one man as competent in the laying out of gardens. He died three years ago and his name was Brown'. Brown himself worked on relatively few Norfolk parks: Holkham, Kimberley, Langley, and Melton Constable. But many more betray signs of his influence. In Brown's reign as 'place-maker' in the second half of the eighteenth century, the fashion was for sweeps of parkland interspersed with circular clumps and a scatter of irregularly-spaced, free-standing trees. The ground was broken by a 'serpentine' stretch of water, and the whole enclosed by tree belts. It was the careful arrangement of water, sweeping contours, and judiciously placed trees, which was now supposed to evoke noble sentiments.

The main problem involved in the creation of such landscapes in Norfolk was the restricting nature of its terrain. As Miss More, writing in the 1750s, put it: 'the charms of nature in this county are of the middling, calm and

33

pacific sort — she does not put forth her bolder, stronger beauties'. In the absence of significant hills and valleys, most attention concentrated on the extent of tree cover, which might serve to redeem the monotony of the agricultural landscape, and also on the use of water.

Figure 10: The Bath House, Melton Constable. A seventeenth-century garden building (compare Figure 4), altered in the eighteenth century, perhaps by 'Capability' Brown.

Arthur Young made a number of comments in his *Six Week Tour* which clearly display contemporary aesthetic preferences, and how far Norfolk landscapes measured up to them. Thus at Melton Constable the park had:

> Lately been ornamented judiciously; and a water made with uncommon difficulty, which, when properly united with wood will have a good effect. From a windmill near the park is a prodigious view of a rich woodland country, finely intermixed with cornfields and wanting nothing but a river to be complete.

Young also commented favourably on Holkham, noting of the lake that it is seen 'through some spreading trees in a most picturesque manner'. Young still looks on the landscape as a composed picture, but his frame of mind is conditioned by the growing propensity to see natural surroundings as the inspiration for fine sentiments. Thus at Houghton he was impressed by the magnificent plantations:

In the road from Syderstone they appear, I think, to the greatest advantage: they are seen to a large extent; with openings left judiciously in many places to let in the view of more distant woods; which changes the shade and gives them that solemn brownness, which always has a very great effect.

Many people commented on the excellence of the plantations at Houghton. But many also pointed out that the park, because of its location, lacked the most essential element of a designed landscape – a lake. This problem was not unique to Houghton. On many sites, the terrain prevented the easy creation of an extensive area of water. This was especially true in the rolling chalk uplands in the north west of the county, and on the flatter, less dissected areas of clay plateau in the south east. At Langley, a lake was proposed by Brown but never constructed, probably because the nature of the terrain would have made it too expensive. At Westwick, elaborate and expensive measures had to be taken to fill the lake, which included the provision of a windmill-driven pump and an aqueduct which ran for many miles through the surrounding countryside.

One of the few parks in Norfolk which really seems to embody the Brownian vision is that at Bayfield. This park originated in the late eighteenth century,

Figure 11: Bayfield Park, near Holt.

35

but was greatly extended in the early years of the nineteenth century. Here, the situation of Bayfield Hall — beside the valley of the river Glaven, cutting through the hills of the Holt-Cromer ridge — provided a fine opportunity for an unknown landscape designer (Figure 11). The slow-flowing river was dammed and widened to create a serpentine lake, and a broad swathe of grassland, scattered with trees, sweeps down to the water. Clumps are placed sporadically on the hillsides to the east, and plantations cover the surrounding hills. In the eighteenth century the driveway led up to the house from the south end of the lake, thus allowing visitors a sustained view of the parkland. In contrast, several of the places in Norfolk where Brown himself worked did not have the kinds of natural advantages enjoyed by Bayfield. At Melton Constable, for example, the parkland is excessively flat, so that the lake he created at considerable expense can barely be seen from the house.

The Picturesque

Towards the end of the eighteenth century, several writers were arguing strongly against such styles of landscape, and the term that came to define their ideals was 'the picturesque'. In 1794 two books were published which popularised the new aesthetic: Uvedale Price's, *Essays on the Picturesque*, and Richard Payne Knight's, *The Landscape*. These new ideas, once again, involved the perception of nature through the medium of the ideal landscape painters, but now the emphasis lay on the creation of rugged, rough surfaces, in contrast to Brown's smooth lines. Such features as hanging cliffs, thundering cascades, wild, wooded hillsides and winding paths were regarded as the prerequisites for a picturesque landscaped scene. Such features were to be arranged in conjunction with the 'three distances' as discovered by the French painters. In the foreground should be placed a formal garden with a terrace, from which the eye should be led to the middle distance where a river or lake should ideally be set. The background should consist of an unremitting outline against the sky, composed of rugged hills covered, if possible, with woods.

In the same year in which these works appeared, Humphry Repton published his *Sketches and Hints on Landscape Gardening*. His designs disappointed the proponents of the picturesque, for although Repton rebelled against the insipidity of Brown's creations, his work still tended towards the mellow nature of Brown's parks, rather than the rugged, raw nature advocated by Knight and Price. There thus followed a protracted, rather bitter dispute about the nature of the picturesque in gardening. One of the ways in which Repton differed from his opponents was that he tended to be more practical, professing that '*utility* must often take the lead of beauty, and convenience be preferred to picturesque effect, in the neighbourhood of man's habitation'. But more important was the kind of commissions he received, and the nature of the raw materials available to him. He worked mainly in the south east of England, where the terrain was muted, and he was often employed by relatively minor landowners. Repton's occasional attempts at creating picturesque scenes in Norfolk were unsuccessful. The grotto he made in an old chalk pit at Holkham, for example, has, not surprisingly, failed to survive!

The factors that prevented Repton from exploiting the picturesque aesthetic have ensured that there is little picturesque landscaping of any kind in Norfolk. The opportunities to exploit scenes of jutting rocks and cascading waters are rare, and Repton and other garden designers had to work with very different, far less amenable, terrain. The situations in Norfolk most suited to the new taste were those near the coast, especially in the hilly countryside between Cley and Cromer. Felbrigg, for example, has fine views, and, before the maturation of the Great Wood, these included glimpses of the sea some three kilometres to the north. At Sheringham, where Repton designed the park, the hall is set in the same coastal hills. From many places within the park, the house can be seen in what, for Norfolk, is a

Figure 12: Sheringham Park, from Repton's *Fragments on the Theory and Practice of Landscape Gardening* (1816).

37

comparatively picturesque setting: wooded hillsides give way to expanses of turf, across which are scattered groups of trees, and once again the sea can be seen in the distance (Figure 12). The house itself is situated against a fine backdrop of trees, though this seems to have been as much for practical as for aesthetic reasons. The trees served to shelter the house from the bitter North Sea winds – a typically Reptonian combination of 'beauty and utility'.

Parks and the Outside World

Although the emphasis throughout the eighteenth century was on the opening up of gardens to the surrounding landscape, from the middle of the century many parks were, in whole or part, confined within shelter belts. These formed frames for the living 'natural' picture. As in the pictures, only selected subject matter was allowed within the scenic space, and in particular anything detrimental to the elevated feelings to be inspired by the landscape had to be removed or hidden. Where a suitably picturesque view existed, especially in the direction of a major valley, the belt might be opened out, as at Bylaugh. Here the hall, to quote the sale particulars of 1917, occupies:

> A Very Fine Position on a sheltered knoll, commanding beautiful and distant views over the finely-timbered slopes of the Park, down into the Valley of the Wensum, forming the nearer portion of this wide Panorama which extends for some miles over a well-timbered undulating countryside.

Little is left of the park now, and the house is itself a picturesque ruin, but the views across the valley can still be appreciated. But here, as elsewhere, the less congenial aspects of the landscape around the hall were hidden from sight, or removed altogether. Kitchen gardens were discreetly screened behind belts of trees, even on occasions moved far from the house. Shelter belts seem to have had as much to do with making the land more private as with picturesque effect. Privacy was all-important, and, as already noted, public roads were closed if they inhibited the view from the park or restricted its expansion. Writing in 1840, James Grigor, author of *The Eastern Arboretum*, noted of Hunstanton:

> Till within a few years, the high road ran very close to the house, greatly circumscribing the park; but the present proprietor, resolving in all ways to make his demesne worthy of the high line

of ancestry whence he derived it, has, at vast expense, created an entire new line of road, at an ample distance from the mansion, and has formed from it an entrance at once easy and natural.

To Grigor, as to most of his contemporaries, there was an intimate connection between the size and privacy of a park, and the nobility of its owner.

Given the difficulties posed by the uninspiring terrain, it is perhaps inevitable that few Norfolk parks fulfilled the landscape ideals established in the eighteenth century. For the most part, social, economic, and practical factors seem to have predominated in the creation of these landscapes. Yet it is, in fact, difficult to appreciate the appearance of most landscape parks during the eighteenth and nineteenth centuries. It is remarkable how much parks have changed even since the 1906 edition of the Ordnance Survey six inch map was surveyed. In particular, many more trees existed in parkland than are present today, and this reduction has greatly diminished the effects of framed vistas and structured contrasts of light and shade. Uninterrupted by trees, many parks are now little more than vast expanses of grassland. At the same time, some trees have grown to a stature which may not have been envisaged two hundred years ago. Whatever the aesthetics determining the design of these landscapes, it is clear we can no longer experience them in the ways that their creators intended.

Chapter Four
Parks and Gardens in the Nineteenth Century

The development of parks and gardens in the nineteenth century was dominated by a reaction against the the static landscaped park, in favour of a greater diversity of styles; and by a renewed interest in the layout of gardens and pleasure grounds in the immediate vicinity of the house. These trends were begun by Humphry Repton, but intensified as the century progressed. Yet the nineteenth century was characterised, not so much by the individual working designer, but by the writers who produced thousands of books, manuals and magazines. A new group of urban middle class rich demanded some of the trappings of taste, but in a form suited to their limited acres. New technology provided the wherewithal – through lawnmowers, cheap glasshouses and the Wardian case – to produce beautiful greenswards, raise extensive ranges of exotic bedding plants, and introduce an even greater variety of non-indigenous plants and trees from the four corners of the world. It was an era of individualism, and diversity.

Repton and Loudon

The first decades of the century were dominated by the figures of Humphry Repton (1752 – 1818) and J.C. Loudon (1783 – 1843). These two set the pattern for the nineteenth century, but in quite different ways – the former as designer and consultant, the latter as writer and propagandist. Repton was, to some extent, the forerunner of the landscape architect, presenting a design concept, which the owner would then employ contractors to execute. Although Repton's 'Red Books' (a report on the site with illustrations, which he presented to the owner) were specific to the location, he was not averse to publishing his ideas in books, thus making them available to a wider public than his elite clients. However, he was very much a garden designer who wrote; Loudon, in contrast, was a writer who also designed. In his prolific career, he produced sixty million words on various gardening subjects, in such publications as the *Encyclopedia of Gardening* and the *Gardener's Magazine*.

Of the two men, it was Repton who had the greatest direct effect on the Norfolk landscape. Born in Bury St Edmunds, he moved to Norwich as a child and at the age of twenty-one set up business as a textile merchant. He traded in the city for a few years before retiring from a career to which he was not ideally suited. He took up residence at Sustead, and lived the life of a country gentleman, reading, painting, and improving his house and garden. But he lacked the resources necessary to sustain this lifestyle, and had again to move, this time to Hare Street in Essex. It was from here that, in 1788, he went into business as a landscape gardener.

Much has been made of the importance of Repton's contacts whilst living in north Norfolk in launching his career. It seems, however, that his business training and relationships whilst in Norwich, and his political work for the Whigs, were of equal importance in providing an entrée into 'society'. His first contract was for Jeremiah Ives, a Norwich textile merchant and leading Whig, and this was followed by work for Thomas Coke of Holkham and, through him, for the Duke of Portland.

Throughout his career, however, Repton worked more for the lesser gentry and the urban upper middle class than for such landed aristocrats. When he did deal with larger sites, his contracts often involved relatively minor alterations to existing parks which had already been landscaped in a Brownian style. At Holkham, for example, his proposals were concerned only with the area around the lake, and much of his work in Norfolk, as at Buckenham Hall, West Tofts Hall, Hanworth and Gunton, was of a similar, rather cosmetic nature.

In his designs Repton utilised a foreground terrace, based, ultimately, on the Italianate garden; a middle ground in the 'natural' Brownian tradition; and a background based on aspects of the countryside beyond the park, carefully selected by judicious breaks in the encircling woodland belts. Within these compositional elements Repton created space for flowers, both indoors in conservatories and outside in beds and trellised enclosures. Repton's style was well suited to the smaller estates of those without the vast acres necessary to create a convincing park on the Brownian model. By using terraces and gardens, the design had more to offer those whose carriage drive was relatively short.

41

One of Repton's biggest disappointments was that he received so few contracts in Norfolk, the place he saw as home. He did, nevertheless, work on nineteen or twenty sites in the county, and these include his first commission, Catton Park, and his last extensive work, Sheringham. No Red Book was ever made for Catton, but it is possible to piece together the nature of Repton's involvement here from a range of evidence. As might be expected of his first work, this was not a revolutionary design, but it does foreshadow some of the characteristic features of his style. The new house and park were to be constructed on a virgin site in a suburban village to the north of Norwich. The house was placed at the top of a rise, with the park spreading out below, towards the city. The basic style was that of Brown: the park utilised existing timber, was partially surrounded by a V-shaped belt of trees, and was separated from the house by a ha ha. But in his treatment of the entrance, the park buildings, and the main view Repton was more innovative. Whereas it had become fashionable to clear all signs of habitation from the vicinity of the park, and to form entrances composed of little split-box lodges in classical style, Repton used an entrance in the village and placed a small rustic house in the grounds. Furthermore, he created views out across the surrounding landscape which were appropriate to the residence: the main vista was of Norwich, where Ives, the owner, had made his fortune, but with a belt strategically placed to obscure the less pleasant parts of the city. Unfortunately, the Catton Park which Repton designed no longer exists, as the site was altered out of all recognition in the 1850s.

Better preserved is Wood Hall, where Repton worked in 1806. As was usual with Repton, the Red Book gave suggestions on how to position the clumps and belts, create a park, place lodges and carriage drives and lay out the garden and woodland walks. However, these were merely proposals which the owner could employ or ignore as he chose. It seems that some of Repton's ideas were utilised, but some – especially those concerning the more distant woodland clumps, the line of the carriage drive, and the entrance lodge – were ignored. The end result was a compact park and garden which utilised thick woodland clumps and broken screens to turn the rather uninspiring and definitely unpicturesque Fenland landscape into an attractive composition. Wood Hall clearly illustrates the dangers of taking Repton's Red Books as a true record of what was actually done; but it is a good example of the kind of small estate which Repton often worked on.

At Sheringham, as at Catton, Repton worked with a virgin site, and in conjunction with the architects building a new house. The commission was dear to his heart: 'this is such a specimen of my art as I never before had an opportunity of displaying ... This may be considered my most favourite work'. He was instrumental both in the choice of site for the house, and in the creation of the landscape, although the potential of the site owed much to the extensive planting carried out by the previous owner of the estate. The Red Book illustrations show how all the components of his style blended to form a scene as artistic as any the eighteenth century could boast. He utilised the undulating land to good effect as his middle ground, formed a suitable garden for viewing the place, and was also able to extend the vista from the approach drives to include glimpses of the sea.

J.C. Loudon was a Scot who came to London as a young man and set up business as a landscape gardener. Most of his major landscaping work was carried out before the 1820s. After this he devoted himself to writing, and to experimenting with garden technology. In his early years as a designer he was a keen advocate of the irregular, picturesque style advocated by Uvedale Price and Richard Payne Knight, but he became increasingly convinced of the value of the formal garden as a work of art. His larger designs thus came to include formal gardens near the house, as well as more picturesque landscaping further away. Although Loudon was, to a certain extent, an imitator of Repton, he was also in part responsible for the rise of what came to be known as the 'Gardenesque' style. This was characterised by the planting of specimen trees and shrubs which were to be looked at and enjoyed individually – a far cry from the wide vistas which had been the epitome of eighteenth-century taste.

Loudon's country house contracts are generally poorly documented, and Norfolk is fortunate in possessing two of his commissions. The first, at Stradsett in 1810, is still the subject of research, but the wealth of documentation has already revealed several interesting features. Here, Loudon was responsible both for the design, and for the supervision of its execution. Stradsett is a large park, and planting continued over several years. The accounts of trees and shrubs purchased at Stradsett in the years 1811 – 15 show an interesting mix of specimen exotic and parkland trees and it would appear that Loudon, like Repton, was experimenting with the use of different types of planting at different distances from the house. Unfortunately, the execution of the commission proved difficult and costly, and was ultimately the source of a law suit with the owner – T.Bagge – over who should be responsible for paying the contractors' fees.

Loudon's other known commission in Norfolk was at Gillingham in 1812

(Plate 7). This was carried out in a very different way. In a rather lengthy introduction, Loudon explains that the plans he had drawn up were 'to enable the proprietor to comprehend and execute the plan with certainty and ease'. Whether his experiences at Stradsett caused him to baulk at overseeing another contract it is now impossible to say; certainly, the plans for Gillingham were made, and the owner left to decide the details of their implementation. Loudon produced two different sets of plans for the site, which he termed the 'ancient' and the 'modern' approaches. The modern style involved a curving drive heralded by entrance lodges, and thick secluding belts of trees which allowed one or two selected views of the surrounding landscape. The ancient proposal featured a regular oval entrance drive, and sunken boundary hedges, which allowed views out into the surrounding countryside. The seventeenth-century formal canal beside the house was to be restored, and American shrubs planted to soften the edges. Louden strongly recommended the ancient proposal, as being in keeping with the character of 'the ancient hall'. In the end, the owner seems to have adopted features of both designs.

The Victorian Garden

Repton and Loudon were undoubtedly influential in re-establishing areas of garden in the immediate vicinity of the house. But they, and subsequent designers in the nineteenth century, were faced with the formidable task of producing designs which successfully resolved a series of conflicting ideas and needs. Society was turning to the past for inspiration in design, and the historical revival in architectural styles, and in particular the enthusiasm for gothic, was followed closely by a similar interest in early gardens. The designed parkland which had formed the setting for great houses in the previous century was not, however, abandoned, but continued to be a vital marker of status. As a result, ways of accomodating both park and garden in one design had to be evolved. At the same time, owners were being influenced by a plethora of tantalisingly illustrated gardening books, magazines, and nurserymen's catalogues, showing the latest plant introductions, rare exotics, and new varieties. The acquisition of such plants became an added status symbol in Victorian society, but they were, for the most part, unsuitable for inclusion in gardens based on seventeenth-century French or Dutch models. The result of these conflicts was an eclectic approach, in which elements of earlier styles were adopted and adapted, but in which very few pure or entire revivals were attempted.

Because there was universal support for the retention of open vistas, the most popular style of garden adopted was the Italianate. Its terracing and ballustrading permitted open views into the park while vases, statues, and fountains provided an acceptable foreground to parkland planting. The open terrace was extremely common, being adopted at Buckenham Tofts, Hillington, Holkham, Melton Constable, Ryston, Wolterton, and elsewhere. Internally, the design of such broad terraces displayed considerable variety. The details at Melton Constable were entirely Italianate, with vases, pedestals, and fountains. At Holkham, however, W.A.Nesfield's design sported a replica of a seventeenth-century French *parterre de broderie*, and as the century progressed planting of terraces became more and more elaborate, as the possibilities of more intricate and colourful bedding were realised. At Hillington, the beds were in the pattern of a Fleur-de-lys flanked by floral representations of the arms of the Ffolkes family. The parterre designed by Lady Lothian at Blickling involved no less than thirty intricately shaped and planted beds. Although this was much simplified in subsequent years, the original layout can still be seen during dry summers, as a pattern of parch-marks in the lawn (Figure 13).

As with the gardens of the sixteenth and seventeenth centuries, only the hard landscaping of the terrace garden — the walls, urns and terraces — usually survives intact. The planting patterns, if they survive at all, have usually been greatly simplified. There are, however, some exceptions, and it is possible to get a good idea of the overall 'feel' of such gardens at a number of sites, and in particular at two which were created by the famous designer W.A. Nesfield.

William Andrews Nesfield was a retired army officer who began a succesful career as a landscape architect in the 1840s, designing gardens in a variety of medieval and Renaissance styles. He often worked in close collaboration with architects employed in the construction, or remodelling, of country houses. At Holkham, Nesfield and the architect William Burn created a formal garden with terraces, pool and fountain, gravel paths and flights of steps. It included a temple and conservatory in a classical style, as well as the massive *parterre de broderie*. At Lynford, he again worked with Burn, who was building a new house in Jacobean-Renaissance style (Figure 14). The gardens were laid out between 1858 − 61 and the design was described by the *Gardener's Chronicle* as one of his largest and best. The gardens were surrounded by low retaining walls, 'with the usual copings for vases' and within were 'the customary terraces with sloping banks of turf, geometrical designs of Box and flower beds, borders, with walks of smashed bricks etc'. The beds were 'well furnished with flowering and foliage plants of the usual

Figure 13: Details of the Victorian gardens at Blickling Hall, revealed by severe parching of the lawn.

character'. The centre-piece was a 'magnificent mistake – two bulls in mortal conflict – which might with great propriety be removed to the forecourt of the mansion'. The design was a classic example of the Victorian historical pastiche, using ideas from a number of differing periods to create a whole which verged on anarchy. At both these sites, the basic framework remains today, although the bedding is much simplified, and at Lynford, the statue of the bulls has been moved!

Although there was some reaction against it in the last decades of the

Figure 14: W.A. Nesfield's magnificent gardens at Lynford Hall, created in the 1860s.

century, this broadly Italianate style continued to dominate the county's larger gardens. There were changes in detail as the gaudier bedding-out plants of the mid nineteenth century gave way to subtler and more long-lasting colours provided by foliage of sub-tropical exotics. But sites like Letton, designed by Edward Boardman, the Norwich architect, in 1882, were still characterised by imposing terraces and geometric beds. The garden designed by G.J. Skipper at Sennowe as late as 1905 is probably the finest remaining Italianate garden in the Norfolk, with terracing on three levels and a plethora of statues by Italian craftsmen (Figure 15).

Figure 15: Part of G.J. Skipper's Italianate gardens at Sennowe Hall, begun in 1905.

Terraces, however, were not the only garden features to appear beside the house in the nineteenth century. The small enclosed ornamental gardens of earlier centuries also experienced a revival, many taking the form of 'theme' gardens of the kind popularised by Repton towards the end of his career. These gardens were invariably placed to the sides of the house or main terrace, and were now usually enclosed by hedges, rather than by walls. James Grigor, writing about Kimberley in the 1830s, noted that 'A terrace 200 yards in length runs along the front of the house. At its western

48

PLATE 5: The great lime avenue at Rougham, planted in the 1690s.

PLATE 6: Humphry Repton's design for the pleasure grounds at Sheringham.

PLATE 7: One of J.C. Loudon's designs for the gardens at Gillingham Hall, 1812.

PLATE 8: Lynford Hall: the magnificent avenue of wellingtonias, planted in the 1860s.

extremity is a flower garden after the old Dutch style'. At Melton Constable in the 1840s, small gardens surrounded by yew hedges were laid out at both the east and north west of the terrace. Heydon also had a formal garden enclosed on three sides by a yew hedge and situated to the west of the hall. By the end of the century, when rose gardens were immensely popular, many of these small gardens were entirely devoted to the cultivation and display of roses, and arbours, open rotundas, and pergolas were prominent features.

As noted in the last chapter, not all country houses in Norfolk lost their walled garden enclosures during the eighteenth century. Where they survived into the nineteenth century, they were suddenly seen once more as objects of beauty, as structures with an antique charm. At sites like Intwood, Mannington, or Kirby Cane, the ancient walls were extensively repaired, and new walls built, complete with crenellations and other details to match the originals.

Perhaps the greatest contribution of the nineteenth century was the introduction of features intermediate between the structured detail of the garden, and the open expanses of the park. Shrubberies and wilderness areas – the latter rather less geometric in layout than those of the previous century – were immensely popular. They provided places to walk, but also shelter for collections of shrubs and the less tender exotics. Paths running through them were bordered with box, yew, laurel (*Prunus lusitanica* and *Prunus laurocerasus*), rhodedendrons, and other evergreens. Similar walks were cut through areas of woodland within the main area of the park.

Many of these features are now badly overgrown, much of the original planting has disappeared, and it is perhaps easy to dismiss them as rather dull and monotonous adjuncts to the nineteenth-century garden. But close examination of maps, plans, and other sources reveals consideable variety in their planting and layout. Thus Stracey's *Norfolk Tour* describes Somerton Hall with 'thriving plantations of oak, chestnut, fir and various other trees, having pleasant walks winding through them. These are planted on each side with roses, jasmine and almost every species of beautiful and flowering shrub. Beyond the walks can be seen the very fine ruins of East Somerton church'. The woodland walks at Intwood were bordered with clipped yew, and arranged to allow a series of glimpses of the park. At Hillington, the wilderness was a roughly circular area to the west of the main gardens. It contained ponds, box-edged serpentine walks, beech and lime standards and a summerhouse 'built in the style of one in Kensington gardens'. At

Blickling, the grove to the east of the hall contained an interesting mixture of regular and irregular walks, and a small hidden geometric garden surrounded by a holly hedge. The overall concept may have been similar, but different sites displayed considerable variety in detail.

More standardised was the display of plant collections. Because their contents were acquired over an extended period of time, the layout of collections usually lacked any overall design. Display was the main aim, and access to distant specimens was more important than the general effect of the planting. Modern technology enabled owners to house the more tender exotics in superb conservatories or winter gardens. Sometimes these were attached to the house, as at Langley, Gillingham, Catton, and Bylaugh, or they could be beautifully engineered, free-standing structures, like that which still exists at Hoveton Hall. Conservatories were expensive to heat and required constant maintenance, so that few have survived the period of 'collectomania'.

The larger shrubs and trees had to be sited outside, and arboreta and pineta were a significant feature of some Norfolk gardens, as described in chapter six. Very few of these collections survive in Norfolk, perhaps because the specimen trees were prone to harsh winters and gale damage. Indeed the effect of the 1987 hurricane on Langley's arboretum is sad evidence of this.

The nineteenth-century garden designers may have been faced with a multitude of aesthetic headaches, but an acceptable compromise was reached, featuring terraces overlooking parkland, smaller enclosed gardens, shrubberies and arboreta, and with woodland walks in the more distant parts of the park. This style, moreover, had the advantage that it could be adapted to sites of almost any size, so that by the end of the century diminutive versions could be found in the larger suburban gardens around Norwich.

Chapter Five
The Kitchen Garden in Norfolk

The least genteel area of the country house landscape was the kitchen garden and, as a result, very little has been written about its history. Only recently has it received much attention, but most writers have concentrated on single examples, usually on large aristocratic estates, on sites worked on by the famous designers, and on the accounts of gardens provided by Victorian manuals and magazines. We still know very little about the majority of kitchen gardens, and even less about the people who worked in them.

Location, Size, and Plan

It is often suggested that when, during the second half of the eighteenth century, Capability Brown and his imitators swept away enclosed gardens from around the country house, the kitchen garden was also banished, far away, to some distant recess of the park. In Norfolk, at least, this conventional account seems to be largely untrue. There are some kitchen gardens, such as those at Bayfield, Beeston St Lawrence, Salle and Narford, which conform to the accepted model. But on the whole, Norfolk has few examples of kitchen gardens built in distant, inconvenient locations. Most remained fairly close to the mansion. Moreover, the exceptions often appeared long before, or long after, the period of Brown's activities. Holkham, Raynham, and Kimberley, for example, gained isolated gardens in the 1720s and 1730s. The distant kitchen gardens at Catton, Didlington, Lynford and Merton, on the other hand, originated *after* the high-point of Brownian 'informality', in the nineteenth century. The majority of kitchen gardens thus stayed close to the house. But they were kept well hidden, usually behind thin belts of trees. Often this secluded location was shared with other unsightly features of the home estate, especially the stables, which were usually located near the kitchen garden in order to facilitate the movement of manure.

Most eighteenth- and nineteenth-century manuals suggested that the kitchen garden should be a rectangular walled structure with its longest walls running east-west, built on ground which sloping gently from north to south. These features were intended to aid drainage, and to maximise the amount of sun received by the crops. Once again, however, Norfolk gardens often deviated from the ideal (Figure 16). Less than half of the gardens studied face due south, most varying in orientation between south east and south west. And while many kitchen gardens were of rectangular form, a significant number displayed quite different layouts. Many adopted a trapezoid or occasionally quadrilateral form, as at Wolterton, Gunton, Hunstanton, Elmham, Heacham, Langley, Hargham, Docking and Gillingham. The most unusual layout is perhaps that at Raynham, where the garden is so trapezoidal in shape that it appears in plan almost as a truncated triangle. Another group of variants had one or more curved walls – examples include Barningham, South Pickenham, Horstead, and Raveningham (Figure 17). At Wood Hall, Hilgay, the gardens are almost oval in plan. In addition, not all kitchen gardens had the full compliment of four walls. That at Ditchingham, for example, only ever had a north and east wall, while at Lexham – where the kitchen garden exhibits a complex pattern of development over several decades – the southern boundary was simply marked by a water-filled ditch. All these unusual gardens appear to have been constructed in the late eighteenth or early nineteenth centuries. After this, plans tended to become more conservative, although the Victorians did occasionally experiment with polygonal shapes, as at Bylaugh and Didlington, both built in the 1850s.

As well as exhibiting considerable variation in their shape, kitchen gardens also varied in size. This seems to have been related to the wealth of the owners, and to the size of their households. Some gardens were really huge: the walls at Holkham, for example, enclose an area of more than six acres (2.1 hectares). This is excessive, however, and in most cases, the walls surround an area of between one and one and a half acres (0.2 – 0.6 hectares). This tells us little about the total area used for the production of fruit and vegetables, however, because in most cases the garden spread outside the confines of the walls. Frame yards, vegetable patches, sometimes entire ranges of glass, as well as orchards and service blocks, could all be found outside the enclosing walls, and sometimes sprawled over an equivalent area.

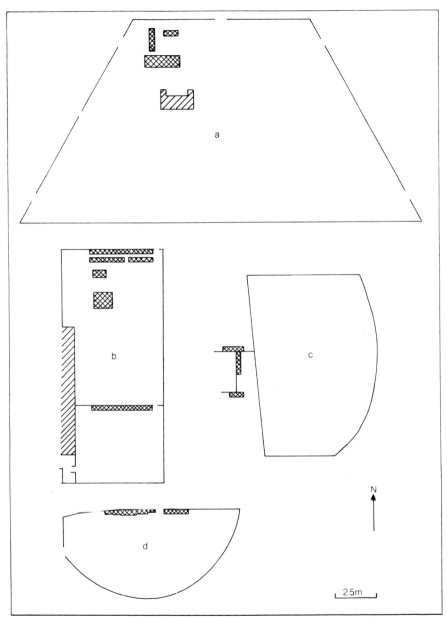

Figure 16: Variations in the size and shape of some kitchen gardens in Norfolk: (a) Raynham (b) Melton Constable (c) Barningham (d) Wood Hall, Hilgay.

Figure 17: Espaliered fruit trees and curved kitchen garden wall, Barningham

The Layout and Use of the Kitchen Garden

Most gardens were laid out with four central plots, divided by walkways, and with further small beds next to the wall. The produce usually included fruit and flowers as well as vegetables. A list of the crops for the kitchen garden at Ryston in the late seventeenth century, for example, mentions salad vegatables such as 'lettice, radishes, scorsa, skirret, spinage, nasturtiums and celery'; conventional roots like carrots, turnips and parsnips; greens like French beans and cabbage; various soft fruits; and flowers, including 'laurell, woodbine, pinkes' and red, white and damask roses. A similar range of plants was still being grown at Felbrigg in the 1780s. Here, the more exotic or attractive vegetables, together with some soft fruit, were planted in the bed under the southern side of the north wall. Under the west wall were the cooking vegetables like cauliflowers, cabbage and sprouts, whilst the bed to the right of the middle walk included herbs, asparagus, cardoons, and brocoli.

The recorder also noted that 'down the middle and cross walks on both sides are borders of flowers', and this was not unusual. In spite of what is sometimes suggested, the kitchen garden, although hidden from sight of house and park, could still be considered a part of the pleasure garden. This seems to have been true throughout the eighteenth century. Bridgeman's plan for Wolterton in the 1720s, for example, shows that the main walkway through the pleasure grounds passed right through the middle of the kitchen garden (Figure 8). At Heydon in the late eighteenth century, the garden was supplied with a summer house, built into the sunny south-facing wall. A particularly impressive summer house, complete with wooden Ionic pillars, was constructed against the south wall of the kitchen garden at Riddlesworth Hall in the early decades of the nineteenth century.

Evidence for the ornamental importance of kitchen gardens is more plentiful from the middle of the nineteenth century. At Intwood, the kitchen garden designed in the last decades of the century was clearly an integral part of the woodland and garden walks. A gravel path ran the full length of the southern end of the garden, terminating at a summer house. A walk back through the garden would have been no less of a beautiful experience for the promenader, who would have passed trained and standard fruit trees, and cultivated plots neatly edged in box.

The *Gardener's Chronicle* correspondent who visited Hillington in 1893 noted that:

> The main walk across the kitchen garden from the vineries and other glasshouses to the retaining wall is furnished on either side with a border devoted to choice herbaceous and other flowers, shut off from the vegatables by espalier Apples and other fruit trees.

Descriptions of Lynford, Gunton and Blickling in this period are very similar, emphasising the importance of flowers, both as decoration for the site itself and for the vases and jardinaires of the house. Kitchen gardens could certainly be thought of as beautiful even if the walled structures which contained them were considered inappropriate in a parkland landscape.

Relatively little is known of the actual management of the gardens before the mid-nineteenth century. Some interesting information comes from contracts made with head gardeners, or from lease agreements. At Stow Bardolph in 1712, for example, the head gardener was expected to keep all 'the gardens, courtyards, orchards and walkes ... according to the best of his skill and knowledge'. He had to 'maintain and keep and furnish ... Stow Hall ... with all necessary and sufficient kitchen garden stuffe ... raise inlay graft and plant as well all sorts of wall fruit, vines and other Fruit ... also all sorts of Greens (as climit will allow) pinkes, tulips and other flowers'. For this and other functions, he was paid £50 per year, and was also allowed to dispose of surplus vegetables for his own profit, although he was expected to supply and pay for his own team of labourers. Later in the century, the usual practice on most medium-sized estates seems to have been to employ a single gardener, who might have a full or part-time assistant, and who could also count on some casual labour, as well as on the help of labourers from the home farm at certain times of the year.

It is clear that few estates, even in the nineteenth century, had the vast teams often shown in the books on great aristocratic houses. A medium-sized estate usually employed a team of three or four gardeners, although male and female labourers would work for a few hours a week in various busy periods. Rates of pay were not good. In 1906, for example, the Heydon estate were paying their five staff wages ranging from 18s per week, through 14s 3d, 12s (13s in summer), to a boy who got 5s.

James Trimbee recorded his experiences as a gardener at Didlington Hall in the early years of this century. The most common labouring activities were digging, hoeing and weeding, especially in the areas growing potatoes. The women did most of the weeding, the casual workers a lot of the digging. The more skilled workers were employed in cutting and planting, both of which were fairly intensive activities in the latter part of the year, whilst in November they had to bring in plants from the pleasure grounds to over-winter in the greenhouse.

Glasshouses and Orangeries

Orangeries emerged in the late seventeenth century, to house the collections of oranges in pots which were fashionable at the time. The orange trees spent the summer outside, but needed to be housed indoors during winter. Orangeries were usually brick-built structures with large sash windows, heated by a furnace or occassionally an open fire. Apart from oranges, they usually housed a range of exotic plants: that at Holkham in 1756, for example, contained oranges, lemons, citrons, and myrtles. Orangeries declined in popularity at the end of the century. Some were simply pulled down, but others were converted to new uses: those at Felbrigg became a Camellia Houses, whilst that at Catton was used to house the owner's collection of stuffed birds!

During the eighteenth century, experiments were beginning with true glasshouses, for forcing fruits and vegetables. The most common was the pinery, for growing pineapples: one was installed at Hillington in the 1770s at a cost of over £300. But although some were erected during the eighteenth century, it was the early nineteenth century which saw their real development, and by the end of the century most kitchen gardens could boast a range of glasshouses. The majority of Norfolk examples were made by the Norwich firm of Boulton and Paul, but they did not have a monopoly. Messenger of Loughborough, for example, provided much of the glass at Melton Constable, while Weeks of London fitted out the new garden at Lynford in 1862. All these firms produced catalogues showing structures ranging from the simplest forcing pit up to the grandest range of houses that money could buy. They produced integral ranges which were usually 'off the peg', erected to standard specifications. Yet there was, nevertheless, scope for customisation, especially in the case of the plant houses, which were used to display the more exotic products of the garden to visitors. These were often very ornate, full-span structures which jutted out from the centre of the range: a particularly fine example still stands in the kitchen garden at Raveningham (Figure 18). Non-standard touches could be subtle and understated, such as the perpendicular arches on the windows of the plant house at Intwood, which echo the arch of the gateway leading into the fruit garden.

Not all estates could vie with Didlington, where in 1910 the glasshouses and associated buildings included: 'Furnace house, peach house in two divisions, range of vineries ... palm house, centre house, orchard and nectarine house and two ranges of six pit lights'. Yet even quite small estates had facilities for producing grapes, melons, cucumbers and peaches, and for raising plants for the house and pleasure gardens all year round.

Within the kitchen garden, glasshouses were usually placed on the south side of the north wall, where they could take best advantage of the sun. Inside, the trees were often planted east-west, giving both sides of the fruit equal exposure to the sun's rays. Vines were planted at the front of the house, where arches were usually provided for the roots to grow outside. To judge from the surviving examples, the majority of houses were lean-tos with simple sloping roofs, although some were three-quarter span (giving extra height and width) and many of the forcing houses were full span, and placed east-west to provide equal amounts of sunlight to the whole growing area. In most kitchen gardens by the end of the nineteenth century, heat was also supplied artificially. The hot water was generated in a boiler house and piped through the main houses in four inch pipes. The boiler house was often placed outside, on the north side of the north wall.

Figure 18: Ornamental glasshouse, Raveningham.

Most glasshouses had a brick-lined walkway, usually around a metre wide, placed near the wall. In the plant houses, however, the walking area would occupy most of the floor space, with benches located around the windows, and with a central wooden stage of three or four levels, on which the plants would be displayed. Forcing pits were designed differently. These were usually sunk a few feet below ground, with the growing area at ground level. The main pit could either be on both sides of a walkway (usual for cucumbers and melons), or else in the centre of the house, with a surrounding walkway (common for pineapples). Forcing pits and frame yards were often placed outside the walls of the garden, as at Raveningham and Gillingham; but if they were located within the enclosure, they usually occupied the area in front of the main ranges of houses. On rare occasions some, or even all, of the glasshouses were located outside the kitchen garden. At Catton and Hoveton, they were part of the pleasure grounds, at Bayfield a vinery was constructed on the outside of the west wall, whilst the enormous variety of glass at Lynford included over one hundred feet of vineries on the outside of the south wall.

Trees

The pride of the kitchen garden, both under glass and outside, was the fruit tree. A wide variety of trees was already available in the seventeenth century: at Ryston, for example, trees grown in the gardens in the 1670s included three varieties of nectarine and four types of peach. Yet the range increased during the eighteenth century, and by the early nineteenth century gardeners devoted many hours to the perfection of fruit from all parts of the world.

Two documents describe the location of different kinds of trees within newly-built kitchen gardens in the middle years of the eighteenth century: one for Honing in 1754, and one for North Elmham in 1765. At Honing, peaches and nectarines were planted against the sunny south-facing wall, while at North Elmham the fruit grown in this location included various dwarf and standard cherry trees, as well as plums and pears. In both gardens, the northern ends of the west and east walls were used for delicate varieties such as greengage and white fig, as well as for nectarines and peaches. In the more shady areas to the south of the garden, however, pears, cherries and plums were the most common fruit. The hardier trees such as apples and pears were grown in shady spots, in the middle of the garden, or outside, against the east or west walls.

In the seventeenth and early eighteenth centuries, fruit trees were either acquired from neighbouring landowners, or bought from commercial nurseries in London. In the 1670s, for example, Roger Pratt of Ryston used the London nurseryman, Leonard Gurle, while in 1754 the garden at Honing was stocked with trees bought from Henry Stevenson's nurseries in Brampton. But as the eighteenth century progressed, firms emerged in Norwich to serve the expanding local market. The most important seem to have been the nurseries run by Aram and by Mackie. Estate accounts are full of references to 'Mackie the gardiner' or 'Aram the seedsman'. By the early nineteenth century, catalogues were becoming common, and as the century progressed, a national network developed, pioneered by Sutton's, whilst firms such as Daniels of Norwich took an increasing share of the market in both the county and the city.

Once bought, fruit trees were carefully tended. They required pruning and tying every year, as well as periodic lifting, and replanting. They also had to be protected from dripping rain, too much sun, frosts and other hazards. Many were *espaliered* — that is, pruned and trained so that their branches grew in one plane (Figure 17). A whole array of products were produced by horticultural engineers to help the gardener in these arduous tasks. Once again, Boulton and Paul were in the forefront, producing glass canopies for the walls, which also served as a support for winter sacking. In the late nineteenth century, the training of trees in the open ground and against walls was made easier by the application of new iron products such as central training frames. The *raidesseur*, introduced from France, allowed trees to be trained without hammering nails into the kitchen garden walls – thus doing away with the holes in the walls, which provided excellent accommodation for red ants!

Espaliers were economical of space, but they were also admired as an aesthetic feature of the gardens. Various styles of training could be employed, and the new frames could be utilised to form blossom arches and fruit canopies along the central walks of the garden. New devices for training trees were only one aspect of a more general proliferation of garden equipment during the nineteenth century. Various types of staging for displaying plants in green houses; bell jars, to protect delicate plants or force others out of season; forcing jars, for sea kale and rhubarb; and a bewildering array of equipment for supplying water to the garden – all these, and more, became available. Partly to accomodate this plethora of equipment, the service buildings connected to the gardens tended to proliferate. At Didlington in 1910, for example, the sale catalogue recorded: 'numerous pot sheds, fruit rooms, an office, tool house, store room, garden stable and coach house, harness room and store shed'.

This was the world the garden staff occupied, not only during the day, but often at night. The head gardener frequently lived in a cottage attached to the kitchen garden, while the unmarried members of his staff sometimes occupied dormitories or bothies nearby. It was here that they worked the wonders of the kitchen garden, producing fruit and vegetables at all times of the year, nurturing plants, and achieving horticultural fame by creating new varieties, such as the famous Blickling Pear. Today, this world is in a state of decay (Figure 19). Some kitchen gardens are totally derelict; the majority are only partially in production. Boilers lie rusting, tool sheds decaying and disused. Most surviving gardens now have only one or two glass houses in operation. The cost of heating and repairing them, combined with the lack of demand for their produce, has meant that most of these fine examples of Victorian engineering have been allowed to fall into decay, or have been demolished.

Figure 19: Derelict glasshouses, Melton Constable. Unlike many such ruins, these are currently being restored.

Chapter Six
Parkland Trees

Trees are the most important component of any parkland landscape, and in most parks a range of species, of widely varying ages, is present. Some trees are survivals from the landscape which existed before the park was created: others reflect successive fashions of tree-planting. Part of the interest and excitement of studying old parks lies in unravelling the complex history of planting on the site.

What makes this task difficult is the absence of a simple, reliable system of ageing trees. The only really accurate method is to count the annual growth rings, but this cannot be done unless the tree has been felled, or a 'core' is taken by drilling. Neither of these options is usually feasible. A rough guide to the age of a tree is, however, provided by its circumference, or girth, measured a few feet above ground level. Allowing for a quicker growth rate in the early years of life, and a slower rate in the more mature stages, most trees with a full crown can be said to have a mean growth of an inch per year. Thus a tree with an eight foot girth is about 100 years old.

However, this rule only applies to free-standing trees. Adjustments have to be made for those planted in avenues, woods, or clumps, which have slower rates of lateral growth. Moreover, certain kinds of tree display marked deviations from this general rule. Some, like the Wellingtonia, the cedar of Lebanon, or the London plane, tend to grow more quickly; others, such as Scots pine, yew, horse chestnut and lime, more slowly. The method can thus only provide a rough guide to the age of a tree. Nevertheless, when combined with other sources of evidence, such as documents, it can provide some useful information.

Figure 20: An ancient pollarded oak in the park at North Elmham.

Pre-Parkland Timber

As already noted in chapter two, many parkland trees in Norfolk are much older than the parks in which they stand. These are usually old oaks, although some ancient beeches can also be found. They often grow on slight banks, which mark the lines of hedges which existed in the landscape before the park was laid out. The hedgerow trees were left standing when the hedges were removed, thus providing the land-owner with 'instant' timber when the park was created. Good examples of this can be found in the park at South Pickenham, which was laid out during the late eighteenth century. A number of relict hedge banks are preserved in the grassland to the west of the hall, on which old oaks and beeches grow. Sometimes, as at Docking, trees stand on banks which once bordered a public road, diverted during the park's formation. Some of the most striking and venerable parkland trees in Norfolk can be found at Raveningham park. The massive oaks must have already been several hundred years old when the park was created, around 1785. Some had once grown in hedgerows, but others seem to have been free-standing pollards in pasture fields. Rather similar are the giant oak pollards in the park at North Elmham, some of which may be more than four hundred years old (Figure 20).

The disposition of existing timber in a landscape may sometimes have helped decide the boundaries of a park. At Honing, for example, an estate map of 1728 shows the area before the park was created. From this it is clear that the belts surrounding the park, shown on William Faden's map of Norfolk of 1797, were partly formed by linking up woods and copses which already existed in the surrounding farmland.

Formal Planting of the Seventeenth and Eighteenth Centuries

Few complete planting schemes survive from the geometric designs of the seventeenth and early eighteenth centuries. Formal avenues, geometric woodland blocks, and groves or wildernesses were usually thinned or altered in the late eightenth century. Enough fragments survive, however, to enable us to ascertain the kinds of trees most commonly used in these designs. The sweet chestnut was particularly popular. It was extensively used at Wolterton, where Charles Bridgeman was consulted about the layout of the grounds in the 1720s. Some ancient sweet chestnuts still stand within areas which were shown as plantations on Bridgeman's plan, which survives in the Bodleian library in Oxford (Figure 8). In addition, their use is expressly stated in a letter written by Horatio Walpole in 1745, which refers to 'a most delightful and innocent army of vegetable striplings of my own raising ... stretching and swelling themselves into timber. They are all of noble and worthy extraction: the names of their families are oaks, Spanish chestnuts, and beech'.

The sweet chestnut also figured prominently in another design attributed to Bridgeman: that of the Grove at Gunton. If this design was indeed by Bridgeman, then it would appear to have been executed some time after his death in 1738, for ring counts on a number of recently felled trees suggest that they were planted in the mid 1740s. Sweet chestnuts were also employed in an unusual grove at Rougham, in which the trees were arranged fan-like, in radiating lines, on either side of a magnificent avenue of lime trees. These sweet chestnuts, which still form an impressive sight, are first shown on an estate map of 1734, and were planted when Sir Roger North built Rougham Hall in the 1690s. Sweet chestnuts planted in the late seventeenth or early eighteenth centuries can be found at a number of other places. At Great Melton, two giant specimens stand in isolation in the park – they may be the remnants of an avenue – while a small grove of gnarled, twisted trees lies on the eastern edge of the park. What is, perhaps, the largest sweet chestnut in Norfolk stands in a small wood to the north of Hanworth Hall. With a massive girth of 29 feet, it is unlikely to have been planted after 1650. Remarkably, it is still thriving.

Sweet chestnuts were occasionally used for avenues, as at Stow Bardolph, where the oldest trees in the avenue running north from the house are of this species. Similarly, isolated specimens in Heydon park suggest that the avenue shown on a map of 1776 consisted of sweet chestnuts. But it was the

Figure 21: The great avenue at Raynham, as drawn by Humphry Prideaux around 1727.

lime that was more commonly used for this purpose. The avenue of limes at Rougham, planted in the late seventeenth century, was aligned on the main facade of the house (itself long demolished), and originally extended southwards through the surrounding fields for nearly a mile. Only a third of the original length now survives, but it is still a fine sight (Plate 5). There has been some replanting, so that trees of widely varying ages now grow side by side, but the oldest of the trees – which have girths in the region of nineteen feet – presumably represent the original planting. The regular replacement of old or damaged trees is a feature of many old avenues, illustrating the care lavished by succesive owners and gardeners over a long period of time. Another fine lime avenue can be seen at Raynham, running south from the hall. This mainly dates from the nineteenth century, but the most southerly trees are probably survivors of the original avenue, planted in the late seventeenth century. Edmund Prideaux's drawing of 1727 shows that the individual trees were originally linked by a high and continuous hedge (Figure 21).

Another tree that seems to have commanded an important place in early eighteenth-century planting is the London plane, probably a hybrid between *Platanus occidentalis* and *Platanus orientalis*, which was introduced to England in 1663. Most surviving examples in Norfolk date from the late eighteenth or early nineteenth centuries, but London planes of earlier date can be seen at Wolterton, Heydon, Kimberley, Ryston and Hillington. Unlike the sweet chestnut or the lime, planes were seldom used in groves or avenues in Norfolk. Instead, they seem to have been treated as a specimen tree, often planted close to the house. The plane has a lighter green foliage than most parkland trees, and is particularly impressive viewed from below, when the twisting pattern of branches can be seen to good effect.

Oak, beech, and sycamore were also extensively employed in these early geometric designs. Oak and beech were, together with sweet chestnut, used in the grove at Gunton. Many of the original trees survive, in good condition. Documentary sources reveal that oak and beech were also used in the grove at Houghton, which was swept away at the end of the eighteenth century. Surviving specimens of lime, beech and sycamore in the park at Docking represent the remains of an avenue shown on an estate map of 1756, and indicate that some early avenues in the county were planted with a mixture of species.

It needs to be stressed that surviving trees provide an unreliable guide to the range of species used in the formal schemes of this period. Documentary evidence indicates that these also made extensive use of conifers. The wilderness flanking the avenue as Raynham, for example, contained not only lime, horse chestnut, hornbeam and other native broad-leafs, but also silver fir, spruce and Scots pine (Figure 21). The trees planted around the summer house at Honing in 1754 included silver fir, arbutus, balm of Gilead fir, Carolina cedar, Lord Weymouth's pine, and larch. None of these trees survives at Honing today.

Parkland Timber in the Late Eighteenth and Nineteenth Centuries

As we have seen, geometric designs gradually fell out of favour during the middle decades of the eighteenth century, and were replaced by the studied informality of the landscape park. As well as making use of existing hedgerow timber, the creators of such parks planted large numbers of new trees, both as parkland timber and in the belts encircling the park. The emphasis was now on the 'natural', and Capability Brown and his contemporaries tended to disapprove of the conifers which had featured in the earlier layouts. Lime and sweet chestnut also lost their prominence. Instead, the dominant tree in parkland, throughout the county, seems to have been the oak. Other trees, such as elm, ash, horse chestnut, sycamore, lime, and Scots pine were also used, but more sparingly. Beech was also planted, but mainly in parks lying in areas of lighter soils, in the north and west of the county.

The woodland in eighteenth- and nineteenth-century parks was not just ornamental. As Tim Stanger discusses in chapter seven, it was also an investment, and managed as an economic resource. Parkland belts and clumps were usually densely planted with a mixture of native hardwoods and conifers. The latter acted as 'nurses', sheltering the slower-growing broad-leaved trees, and were repeatedly thinned as the years passed, providing a steady income. The hardwood timber, in contrast, was regarded as a longer-term investment. In addition, many belts contained coppiced trees, the poles from which not only provided a steady income but also the material for hurdles etc., used on the home farm of the estate.

Exotic Planting in the Nineteenth Century

From the late eighteenth century, changing tastes and an increasing number of introductions meant that large numbers of exotic species were planted in Norfolk parks, usually in the immediate vicinity of the house. Many different species can be found, but among those most widely planted were the cedar of Lebanon, the monkey puzzle, and the Wellingtonia.

The cedar of Lebanon had been used in early geometric designs, and continued to be planted near country houses throughout the century. Thus, for example, the fine specimen growing beside Raynham Hall seems to have been planted during the second half of the eighteenth century. The cedar increased in popularity during the nineteenth century, and many Norfolk country houses are graced by fine examples of this tree, including Intwood Hall, Ditchingham Hall, and Stow Bardolph (Figure 22). Not all were planted close to the house. They can also be found out in the parkland, although seldom in the more distant recesses, or within the belts. One important exception to this general rule is the park at Hunstanton, where groves of cedars, and a mixed grove of cedars, monkey puzzles, and coast redwoods, can be found more than a kilometre from the hall.

Figure 22: Cedar of Lebanon, Intwood Hall.

The Wellingtonia was widely planted in Norfolk parks and gardens during the second half of the nineteenth century, and in a variety of situations. A tall, narrowly conic tree, it can grow to a height of 250 feet in its native California, and live for 3,000 years. In Norfolk, Wellingtonias usually appear as isolated specimens in parkland, as at Raynham, Catton, Gillingham or Heacham. Sometimes, however, they were used as the main trees in a

68

shrubbery, as at Heydon, while at Lynford they were planted as an avenue. Now huge and sombre, the latter trees superbly compliment the 'Jacobethan' architecture of the house (Plate 8). If, as seems likely, the avenue was planted around the time that the house was built, in 1862, then the owners were in the forefront of contemporary fashion, for the Wellingtonia had only been introduced to England some nine years earlier.

The monkey puzzle was introduced in 1795 from Argentina and was widely planted in shrubberies or in the immediate vicinity of the house, but also occasionally in the open parkland, as at Hunstanton or Barningham. Particularly fine examples can be seen in the parks at Letton, Gunthorpe and North Elmham.

The introductions of the nineteenth century vastly increased the range of trees available to landowners. Altogether, a total of sixty-eight different species has so far been recorded in Norfolk parks and gardens. Among many of note for their rarity or magnificence, mention should be made of a fine chestnut-leaved oak in the parkland at Rougham, the stone pine at Gillingham, the much-propped cork oak at Melton Constable and the unusual fastigiate oaks at Buckenham Tofts.

Arboreal Gardens and Arboreta

An important feature of some nineteenth-century parks was the arboreal garden. These were planted with a number of exotics, but in association with indigenous species. The trees were allowed room to grow as specimens, in line with the ideas of J.C.Loudon. In some gardens of this type, the trees were underplanted with shrubs, or flower borders. The arboreal garden at Ryston hall, which is only now reaching its best, is probably the most botanically interesting in Norfolk. Old London planes provide the basis for the planting, which includes Atlas cedar, cedar of Lebanon, cut-leaved beech, swamp cypress, white poplar, silver birch, narrow-leaved ash, coast redwood, Douglas fir, American red oak, catalpa, and false acacia. There is also a walk lined with varieties of *acer palmatum*, and numerous dwarf rhododendrons.

The garden at Langley is in similar style and was, to judge from contemporary photographs, at its peak in the 1930s. Cedars provide the framework for the design, which incorporates monkey puzzle, Bhutan pine, Wellingtonia, holm oak, Corsican pine, and Irish yew, as well as the more usual indigenous species. Stow Bardolph has another magnificent example of this kind of garden. In this case, most of the trees are set in grass, with no accompanying flower borders or shrubbery. Cedars again provide the basic framework, in association with good specimens of oak, sycamore, lime, beech and horse chestnut. There are also four London planes, and an outstanding cut-leaved beech which has branches radiating to the ground, subsequently rooting and forming a magnificent arbour nearly 100 feet in diameter. Other species present include holm oak, hedgehog fir, weeping beech, weeping ash and — a surprising find for Norfolk — two gingkos in good condition.

There is some dispute as to whether gardens like this really deserve the title of 'arboreta'. Strictly speaking, this term should really be reserved for scientific collections, in which the trees are grouped according to species and variety, rather than for aesthetic effect. Perhaps the only true nineteenth-century arboretum in Norfolk is that at Ryston, apparently planted at the very end of the century. A plan showing the species present was made in 1913, and it is noteworthy that less than a third of the trees listed still survive today — perhaps a consequence of the county's exposure to cold north-easterly winds.

Parkland Trees Today

The plantations and woodland belts within and around parks are very varied. Often they are dominated by oak standards, usually around 100 to 150 years old, sometimes accompanied by old coppiced hazel. Another common type consists of a mixture of oak, beech and sweet chestnut standards. There are occasional oddities: one mid nineteenth-century belt at Hunstanton is composed entirely of holm oak. Whatever their original nature, however, most parkland plantations and belts are changing. Most are being invaded, to a greater or lesser extent, by sycamore; and many have been replanted with areas of commercial conifers. Many owners are, however, also replanting sections of belts with indigenous hardwoods, especially oak.

Today, the dominant free-standing timber tree in Norfolk parkland is the pedunculate oak. In some parks, such as Gawdy in Redenhall, there are hardly any other species, but this is unusual. More usually, oak is accompanied by some combination of beech, horse chestnut, lime, sweet chestnut and sycamore. Scots pine, hawthorn, ash, silver birch, Turkey oak, willow, and poplar are also often present.

There have been important changes in the composition of parkland timber during the last century. Elms, once common in Norfolk parks, have almost entirely disappeared due to the ravages of Dutch elm disease. Ash, less long-lived than oak and more prone to gales, is also much less prominent than it was in the nineteenth century. The most significant change has, however, been the overall reduction in the number of trees standing in parks. Even where parkland has remained under grass, and not been converted to other uses, reduction has often been on a massive scale: it is not unusual to find a park which contains only 30% of the trees shown on the 1906 Ordnance Survey six inch map. This general situation was not improved by the gales of October 1987, which felled large numbers of trees. In many parks, moreover, the trees which do survive are now getting old, and vulnerable. Many owners have taken steps to remedy this situation, and have been carrying out extensive schemes of replanting. Nevertheless, a large number of parks are now little more than areas of pasture, rather sparsely scattered with gale-damaged and over-mature trees.

Chapter Seven
Parkland: Recreation and Exploitation

Most books about the landscape parks of the eighteenth and nineteenth centuries concentrate on their design and appearance, on their status as 'works of art'. But this is only part of the story. Parks were created not only to be looked at, but also to be enjoyed, and they were used for a wide range of recreational activities. They also had a number of important economic functions, which are also usually ignored in works on garden history.

At the most basic level, parks could be used for walking or riding. Thus in 1728, Matthew Decker visited Robert Walpole at Houghton, and described how 'we went on horseback round about the grounds and Park, where he showed me what was done already, and what is more designed, and among the rest we rode through a wood of oaks and beech'. Similarly, in 1788, Sylas Neville described a visit to Holkham:

> Wed.Morning, Aug.6. Went what they call the home circuit, with some of the ladies and gentlemen. This is a little tour to see the grounds, different vistas etc. The park when the plan is completed will be 11 miles round. Rode on horseback.

Because walking and riding in parks were everyday activities, they are seldom commented on in documents. They are usually mentioned obliquely, in comments about some other matter.

Deer

As already noted in chapter two, prior to the eighteenth century the word 'park' meant an enclosed area where deer were kept, both for the meat they provided and for sport. A park full of deer conferred a particularly aristocratic air to the mansion standing within it. Deer had always had elite associations, and these were augmented by the vicious anti-poaching legislation of the 1720s, the notorious Black Acts, which made it illegal to buy or sell venison on the open market. Deer were thus taken out of the market place, and venison became, to some extent, an article of 'gift exchange': a special present which could be given as a reward for political support or other favours. Venison was, however, also sold to neighbouring gentry families, and the account books of James Coldham of Anmer, and of the Rolfe family at Heacham, contain numerous entries relating to payments for deer. Those for Heacham reveal that, between 1764 and 1817, the price of venison remained remarkably stable, at a guinea for a buck, and 10/6 for a doe. The deer came from both Houghton and North Elmham, and it is noticeable that purchases were almost always made between late summer and Christmas. Interestingly, most of the purchases from Houghton occurred in September, while those from Elmham were made in August, presumably reflecting the different culling patterns on the two estates.

Deer continued to be kept at many sites throughout the eighteenth century, and even in the middle years of the nineteenth century they were occasionally introduced into landscape parks, as at North Elmham, or Castle Acre. Today only a handful of parks, including Holkham, Melton Constable, and Houghton, are still stocked with deer.

Water

Fish ponds were common in the medieval landscape, and were a feature of many deer parks. Two such ponds survive in the park at Melton Constable, the remnants of an impressive sequence, arranged in steps down the side of a hill, which is shown on a map of 1673. Kip and Knyff's illustration of 1707 (Figure 4) shows that they were later used as a feature in the great geometric gardens which had, by this time, been laid out around the hall. Nevertheless, they were probably still stocked with fish. Fish ponds continued to be maintained, and constructed, in many parks and gardens in the first half of the eighteenth century. They usually took the form of rigidly geometric squares and rectangles, and it is difficult to tell how far this was for functional reasons, and how far it was a reflection of contemporary fashions in garden design. A map of Merton park, dated 1733, shows a particularly complex arrangement of rectangular ponds, with three, roughly parallel ponds enclosed by a five-sided, moat-like feature. This arrangement was destroyed in 1757, when it was transformed into the more irregular areas of water that exist there today. These new ponds were expensive features: the

Great Pond alone cost £110 to construct. The importance of ponds in estate management is indicated by a headstone in the churchyard at Gunton, which now lies within Gunton Park. The inscription to one John Briggs, who died in 1709, states that he was the 'head pond maker to John Harbord', owner of Gunton hall.

Documents from Heydon and Merton provide some details of the management of park ponds in the eighteenth century. At Heydon in 1740 the owner was putting 20 brace of tench into the 'small new square pond in the garden', 20 brace of very small carp into the moat, and 30 brace of gudgeon into the 'largest new square pond'. In the case of Merton, the fish books of Thomas de Grey describe in some detail the number and type of fish put into the various ponds: carp and perch in the great pond, pike in the garden pond. Evidently the work was accomplished by trial and error, and de Grey found certain fish unsuitable for certain ponds. The importance of the ponds and their fish is well illustrated by the opening words of the new fish book begun by de Grey in 1778:

> Having kept an account of my fish in different ponds and waters from may 1762, at which time i began to stock and attend to them, and that account now growing confused by its variety, i have reduced it to a smaller compass for the amusement of those who may succeed to a place which is not without those advantages so necessary for the comfort of a country life.

As this implies, fish ponds were maintained for a mixture of motives: functional, aesthetic, and as a hobby suited to the life of the rural squire. This combination could produce bizarre results: at Buckenham Tofts in the late seventeenth century the new fish pond was built on top of the house!

Water was an important ornament in the landscape parks of the eighteenth and nineteenth centuries, in the form of serpentine lakes or irregular water courses. Besides providing ice for the ice house and, often, water for the mansion, they were also stocked with fish. In the nineteenth century, sales catalogues frequently drew attention to the quality of the fishing. Sennowe had 'capital trout fishing', North Elmham advertised 'good fishing in the lake, the river and various streams on the estate', while Didlington claimed 'excellent trout stream and lake. The river Wissey is well stocked with coarse fish'. More exotically, there was also the lure of otter hunting in the lake.

Areas of water within parks had other uses. Several eighteenth- and

Figure 23: The boat house, Sennowe Hall.

nineteenthth-century illustrations show rowing or sailing boats in use on parkland lakes, and boat-houses often figure on old maps. Surviving boat-houses, however, usually appear to be of early twentieth-century date. At Sennowe, the boathouse, situated at the western end of the lake, is a picturesque timbered building, which originally had a thatched roof (Figure 23). At Didlington it is an underground structure with a curved vaulted roof, located beneath the tennis courts, and reached by an imposing flight of ballustraded steps (Figure 24).

Some areas of water within parks were used as duck decoys – trapping grounds for wildfowl. Decoys were an important feature of the Norfolk landscape until the early part of this century. At Wretham Park, a natural area of water known as Micklemere was converted into a decoy in 1836, by the addition of the characteristic netted funnels, down which the birds would be lured. In the 1870s, an average of over 800 wild-fowl were being taken there each year. Gunton, Didlington, Narford, Hillington and Westwick also had functioning decoys in the nineteenth century. With the increasing importance of shooting on estates, however, as the nineteenth century progressed, decoys were gradually rendered redundant. The use of guns tended to scare wildfowl away from them. Moreover, they needed efficient management to remain successful. At Westwick the average yearly take for the seventeen years up to 1886 was 409, but previously it had been closer to a thousand. The reason for this decline given in estate records is that the man who worked the decoy was not trained, and did not employ a proper decoy dog. At Wretham the owners found that if there was an abundance of acorns the ducks would wander off into the game plantations.

Figure 24: The boat house, Didlington Hall, from an old postcard.

Shooting

The rise of the shooting estate in Norfolk is sometimes thought of as a phenomenon of the late Victorian period, associated with Prince Edward's well-known predilection for the sport. But of course, shooting was an important pastime for the landed rich from the sixteenth century, and estate records from Hunstanton show that game was being killed there with the gun as early as 1533. Shooting did, however, gradually increase in importance during subsequent centuries, partly because of the spread of enclosure and the consolidation of large landed estates. This made it easier for landowners to maintain a stock of game, without the risk of it wandering off onto someone else's property. By 1727, a description of Heydon, written when the estate was to be leased, spoke in glowing terms of 'a good swannery, plenty of all sorts of game, as also wild fowl, plovers, curlews, wheatears'.

During the second half of the eighteenth century, game books show that large amounts of game were being taken in parks, and on the surrounding estate land. At Hillington during the 1772 – 3 season, the 'bag' consisted of 493 partridges, 110 pheasants and 49 hares. It is noteworthy that a good proportion of these were distributed as gifts throughout the neighbourhood. At Merton, too, much of the game taken was given away, sometimes in return for favours: as late as 1866 a local brickmaker complained to Lord Walsingham that he was still waiting for the game he had been promised in return for his vote !

In his travels around Norfolk during the last decade of the eighteenth century, William Marshall noted that the 'ornamental plantations, about the residences of men of fortune, are here, as in other districts fashionable; not, however, as objects of ornament merely, but likewise as nurseries of game'. The belts and clumps associated with a landscape park were an ideal place for rearing game birds, providing both shelter and protection from poachers. By the middle of the nineteenth century the great majority of Norfolk parks, like the surrounding estate land, would have been stocked with game.

But as the nineteenth century progressed the sport was changing. From the 1850s technological improvements in gunmaking followed rapidly on the heels of the first breechloaders. Organised driving began around 1860, first probably at Holkham. Pheasants began to take over from partridges as the dominant species of game, partly because they were easier to rear in large quantities. As the sport became more organised and sophisticated, the quantities of game bagged spiralled. In 1802 what was then claimed to be 'the greatest day's sport ever known in Norfolk', took place at Houghton. The bag was 165 hares, 42 pheasants, 5 rabbits, a woodcock and two partridges. This was a paltry total compared to what would be shot at places such as Holkham, Sandringham, Merton and Quidenham towards the end of the century.

The sport on an estate could be an important source of income. As early as 1823 the shooting rights at Heydon were being leased for £240 a year. With the agricultural depression of the 1870s, the letting of shooting rights became a financial necessity for some estates, particularly those in the more marginal agricultural areas in the west of the county. As Lord Walsingham, the owner of Merton, told Rider Haggard, the owners of estates in the Breckland area were able to 'muddle along' simply on the proceeds from the sporting amenities, for: 'the majority of owners in that district would receive no advantage from their land if not for its suitability to the purpose of game rearing'.

But sport could also have less welcome effects in this period. especially on those larger estates which had the dubious privilege of entertaining the royal entourage. The Merton estate suffered dramatically from Lord Walsingham's generosity towards his royal guest, and in particular from the ability of the Prince's retinue to drain a 300-year-old wine cellar in a matter of days. This did nothing to help the wider economic problems facing the estate at the time, problems which eventually led to the sale of outlying farms.

Forestry

As well as providing recreation and sport for their owners, parks had a number of more prosaic economic functions. The woodland within landscape parks did not simply form an element in an aesthetic landscape, and provide shelter for game. It was also systematically exploited for timber. Wiggins, the steward at Stow Bardolph, stressed the combined functions of woodland in his survey of the estate in 1809:

> On so extensive an estate it is highly advisable to encourage the growth of the more valuable kinds of wood as Oak, Ash, Elm and Chestnut and in large masses — the immediate advantages of this kind of improvement are not inconsiderable as to ornament, game, shelter etc and the returns though distant are sure to be large under proper management.

That 'proper management' was subsequently instituted is shown by the rapid rise in the income from timber on the estate. In 1775 this amounted to just over £22 per annum, but by 1872 it had risen to over £407. Not all of this woodland was in the park itself, of course, but much of it lay in the northern perimeter belts. Nor was all the wood produced actually sold. The accounts for 1863, for example, show that the value of poles and hurdles cut on the estate came to almost £838, but £377 worth of this was used on the estate itself, especially for making hurdle fences.

Here, as on other estates, the poles and underwood showed a regular profit: timber sales were more variable. There was some regular thinning of the conifer timber which was usually planted in among the hardwood trees in the belts, but most of the hardwood timber seems to have been considered as a long-term investment. The free-standing trees in the parkland do not

78

seem to have been considered in primarily economic terms, although even these could be felled if money was needed quickly. Thus at Merton in 1857 a large number of old trees were auctioned off:

> The auctioneer respectfully solicits the attention of shipbuilders, wheelwrights and the public in general to this important and unreserved sale of timber. Many of the oak trees are of long lengths and large dimensions, remarkably fine, of a superior quality, and most conveniently situated for removal.

Farming

Although ostensibly divorced from the practicalities of farming, all parks were to some extent exploited agriculturally. Grazing had to take place, in order to keep the grass down, and engravings and drawings of Norfolk seats in the eighteenth and nineteenth centuries often depict a few sheep or cattle grazing somewhat idyllically within the parkland. This, however, was as far as contemporary attitudes would allow agriculture to impose itself on the designed landscape. Several parks, including Holkham, Hoveton, and Langley, had home farms within their perimeter belts, but these were discreetly screened by clumps or belts from view of the house. Areas of arable land, and farm buildings, were both to be avoided. As the steward of Stow Bardolph advised in 1809:

> Provide and set out a suitable farm or park to be kept in hand with the mansion of Stow hall sufficiently large to maintain the required stock of cows and sheep and provide hay for the stable, but carefully avoiding an extension of the farming establishment beyond these objects, under the consideration that nothing but the gratification of a great partiality to agricultural pursuits can recompense a gentleman for the losses and vexations he almost always suffers from an extensive farm in hand. This being particularly the case with arable land, it was determined to lay down to grass all such land as approached too near the mansion.

Not all of the smaller estates in the eighteenth and nineteenth centuries could afford this careful separation of aesthetics and agriculture, however. James Grigor, writing in 1841, was strongly critical of Hillington:

> Here ... we have farm-buildings, stacks of straw, groups of

working-horses, all in full view upon entering the park, and nothing of that refinement indicated by the appearance of the entrance-gate.

This was a situation which few landowners with any pretensions to gentility would have allowed, however great their interest in agriculture. Even at Holkham, famed for its owners' advocacy of agricultural improvement, farming activity was hidden away from the house. Although the majority of landowners made their wealth from agriculture, visitors to their parks did not expect to be confronted by views of capital accumulation in action.

Parks Today

As long as agriculture was buoyant, appearances could be kept up. The great period of park expansion and country house building in Norfolk took place between 1770 and 1860, when the returns from agriculture were, for the most part, booming. The agricultural depression which started in the 1870s, however, saw the beginning of the end of the landscape park. Many estates were badly affected by decling rents, and the last decades of the century saw many sold off (Figure 25).

The agricultural depression was accompanied by other social, political and economic trends which ensured that the country house and its park were no longer the prime expressions of wealth and status. Norfolk today has more surviving parks than most counties, but even so many have disappeared since the beginning of the century. Their fates have been diverse.

In some cases, the park has disappeared because the country house has also gone. Buckenham Tofts Hall was demolished at the end of the Second World War and the park, although still a recognisable feature of the landscape, is part of the Battle Training Area. At Wretham the hall has also gone, but here the park has entirely disappeared, its former area a mixture of agricultural land and stud farm. At Bylaugh, the house still survives as an impressive ruin, but the park is entirely under the plough. In contrast, in a few cases, such as Gawdy Park in Redenhall, or Heacham, the house has disappeared and yet the parkland still survives.

In a number of other places country houses have survived, but with a changed use. Where this has happened, the park has sometimes also survived, sometimes not. Letton Hall is now used as a Christian conference centre and the park is let as farmland. Lynford Hall is now a hotel, with the gardens and part of the park maintained for the enjoyment of the guests. Gunton Hall is in divided occupancy, and only part of the park maintained. At Melton Constable, the hall is being converted to residential and business use, and the gardens are being restored, but the park with its deer are under separate ownership. Catton is a nursing home, and most of the grounds are under the plough. Quidenham Hall is now a nunnery, and only the area of the park near the house survives. Langley Hall is a school, and much of the park is arable farmland; of the remainder, some is maintained as ornamental grounds but large areas are given over to playing fields.

Where country houses remain in the occupation of private families, the usual pattern is for the area of parkland near the house to be maintained, while the more distant areas are returned to the plough, as at Raynham, Docking, Elmham, Hanworth or Stradsett. At Ryston, the more distant areas of the park have been converted into a golf course. Perhaps most bizarre of all, much of the park at Weston Longville has been made into a Dinosaur Theme Park, and life-size examples of Tyrannosaurus Rex and Iguanadon lurk in the clumps and plantations. Blickling, Felbrigg, and Sheringham are now owned, and beautifully maintained, by the National Trust.

Even where parks have been damaged or destroyed, they can still have an important impact on the landscape, their belts and plantations often the most conspicuous features in an increasingly treeless countryside.

FIRST EDITION.

BY ORDER OF THE MORTGAGEES.—IN NINE LOTS.

NORFOLK,

IN THE PARISHES OF GREAT RYBURGH, LITTLE RYBURGH, GUIST, ELMHAM, GATELEY, STIBBARD,
PUDDING NORTON, TESTERTON AND COLKIRK.

PARTICULARS
OF

The Sennowe Estate,

A HIGHLY IMPORTANT

RESIDENTIAL & SPORTING DOMAIN,

ALL FREEHOLD AND PART TITHE FREE,
AND COMPRISING

SENNOWE HALL,

ATTRACTIVELY SITUATED AND OF MEDIUM SIZE,

CHARMING BUT INEXPENSIVE PLEASURE GROUNDS,

WELL-TIMBERED PARK, BEAUTIFUL WOODLANDS & PLANTATIONS,

FORMING FINE GAME COVERTS,

NUMEROUS COMPACT FARMS,

WITH UNUSUALLY GOOD RESIDENCES AND EXTENSIVE HOMESTEADS,

All Let and in good Order,

SEVERAL EXCELLENT COTTAGES AND LODGES,

A GENTLEMAN'S RESIDENCE AND GROUNDS.

THREE WELL-SECURED GROUND RENTS,

A VALUABLE WATER MILL AND OTHER PREMISES,

THE WHOLE COMPRISING NEARLY

4,400 Acres,

PRODUCING A REDUCED RENTAL OF UPWARDS OF

£6,000 PER ANNUM,

AND OFFERING AN UNUSUALLY SOUND HIGH-CLASS INVESTMENT;
WITH

*The MANORS of Great Ryburgh, Woodhall in Little Ryburgh, Stibbard, Ryburgh Paveless,
and Little Ryburgh Horsham St. Faith's; the Advowsons of the Rectories of Testerton and
Pudding Norton:*

The Property will be offered in 9 Lots, of which Lot 1 comprises a beautiful and compact SPORTING
and RESIDENTIAL ESTATE of about 1,527 Acres.

The Hall is situate about 2 miles from Ryburgh Station on the Line from Wymondham to Wells, 4 hours from London,
about 5 miles from the Market Town of Fakenham, where are Stations on the Great Eastern and Eastern and Midlands
Railways; Wells, East Dereham, King's Lynn and Norwich are within easy reach, and in the neighbourhood are the Seats
of many of the best Norfolk Families:

Figure 25: Detail from a sale catalogue for Sennowe Hall, 1887.

82